BEYOND THE MIND

CONVERSATIONS

ON THE

DEEPER SIGNIFICANCE OF LIVING

BY

DADA

San Francisco
California

Copyright © 1977 by Dada
c/o Dada Center
13665 Foothill Avenue
San Martin, CA 95046

DADAJI
'TAPOVAN', (NEAR RAM MANDIR),
YEVOOR, P.O. BOX NO.-3,
THANE - 400 601. (INDIA).
PHONE : 544 71 05.

All rights reserved. No part of this book may be reproduced in any form without permission from the publisher, except by a reviewer who wishes to quote brief passages in connection with a review written for inclusion in magazine or newspaper or radio broadcast.

First printing: September 1977

Library of Congress Catalog Number   77-85723

International Standard Book Number

    clothbound: 0-930608-00-3
    paperbound: 0-930608-01-1

Drawings: Rick Wheeler
Cover Design: Bob O'Connor
Calligraphy: Sahnta Pannutti
Typesetting: Penguin People, Santa Clara, CA.
Printing: Joel Shefflin, Peter G. Levison Assoc., San Francisco, CA.
Color Separation: Paddy McLennan, Focus 4, Belmont, CA.

MANUFACTURED IN THE UNITED STATES OF AMERICA

ACKNOWLEDGMENTS

I cannot forget, Ken Reed, how you very boldly made the first tape recording of one of my talks without my knowledge! And that proved to be the beginning of the recordings of the interviews and talks thereafter. Thank you.

Later during the lecture tour in Los Angeles and San Francisco, the interviews and talks were tape recorded. But to bring the tapes in book form, a lot of work was necessary. And without the help of some of my friends, the transition of tapes into a book in a short time would have been impossible.

I remember, Markell Brooks, how you started the ball rolling by transcribing the first tape yourself in your home in Pacific Palisades. Without your encouragement and benevolent insistence, I would not have thought of beginning this book. You are greatly responsible for initiating this project.

Ira Flushman, I am grateful for your enthusiastic work in transcribing the tapes and helping with the editing. Judith Scott and Sondra Bennett, your helping hand in transcribing the tapes is very much appreciated.

Helen and Carroll Wright, you both gave me useful assistance in putting together the transcribed material. Your help at various stages was invaluable.

Bob Hutchins, your keen interest in this publication, and your readiness to assist at various stages of the book, was surely very encouraging.

Raj Mehta, your overall management of the project, and your assistance in editing, have been indispensable.

Nancy Lloyde, you have played an important part in overall editing of the book, and your skillful and untiring work with dedication in typing the manuscript in a short time has surprised me. Your help made the completion of the book possible.

Juanita Gilbert, it was so good of you to look after all those who came to work on the book in your home at 25 Bolinas Avenue. Also your help in editing is greatly appreciated.

Rick Wheeler, you have done a magnificent job of bringing the essence of the chapters into the charcoal drawings. You have worked with the feelings and modesty of an artist, as well as with the devotion of a seeker.

Bob O'Connor, I am pleased with the personal interest you took in designing the cover. It was a job well done.

Jean Allen, Leigh-Taylor Young, Bob Carr, Conrad Keeler, Steve Bruce, David Hoffman, Larry Swan and Brenda Sales, Ron Ruffkin, Jessica and Jilly — you all have had a share in assisting with this book.

DADA

CONTENTS

Acknowledgments   iii
Preface   vi
A Word to the Reader   vii
About the Author   viii
Freedom from Time   1

1. **THE SEEKER**   2
   (The Way)
   What is the way of attaining liberation? How can I live and work in the spirit? Who will show me the path?

2. **THE FAMILY MAN**   22
   (The Play)
   What is love? How can I love my relatives and friends? How should a family man approach sex? Has sex any higher purpose and significance in life?

3. **THE PSYCHOTHERAPIST**   36
   (Flowering)
   How can I help others solve their emotional and psychological problems? What is healing? Is it possible to change the mind? How does spiritual understanding relate to daily problems?

4. **THE WEALTHY PERSON**   60
   (Imprisonment)
   Why does being rich prevent me from being happy? Is wealth an impediment to attaining spiritual freedom? Is there such a thing as peace of mind?

5. **THE RESEARCHER** 72
    (Maze)
    Is it not a fact that through scientific research and conclusions we can educate and change the world? Don't we need more information to convince people? Would you cooperate in measuring spiritual energy in the lab?

6. **THE ARTIST** 90
    (Expression)
    What is true art? How can I find my creative energy? Are talent and technique necesary for the discovery of creativity?

7. **THE WOMAN** 104
    (Ascent)
    Are my feminine emotionality and sensitivity blocks to a higher consciousness? Are devotion and faith necessary for spiritual progress? Is it possible to be free from sexual energy?

8. **THE MEDITATOR** 122
    (Liberation)
    What is meditation? Is it necessary to live in a religious community to achieve spiritual growth? What are fear and loneliness? Is suffering an inherent part of the spiritual search?

Fulfillment 135

PREFACE

Dada arrived in the United States in September of 1975. During his first year of touring in California and Washington, people from many different professions, faiths and lifestyles somehow found themselves in quiet discourse with this unusual man. Despite their educational qualifiactions and material successes, most of them had no awareness of what Dada refers to as "the true significance of living." They seemed to be caught in a web, kept away from the peace and fulfillment that they struggled and searched for by the very path on which they sought to find them.

Each chapter in this book is a conversation with one of these individuals: a person living as a specialized human entity in society, painfully alone and yet imprisoned by a self-made mold of education, profession and aspiration. These eight discussions are representative of the many Dada has held with psychologist and biophysicist, musician and movie star, family man and millionaire, artist, mother, student and so many more.

As months passed, a few close to Dada shared informal evenings with him, and the idea of this book slowly came into being. People who spent time with Dada became able to penetrate with understanding the illusive nature and limitations of their "mind game." They became aware of the walls of their own prisons, and glimpsed the possibility of going beyond the mind toward freedom, which Dada kept gently and persistently telling us is "the liberation of life." As we heard and saw and felt and understood, a momentum gathered for the compilation of Dada's teachings in book form. Dada spent many months reviewing miles of tape and hundreds of pages of transcript. Helpers gave their time, skills, and whatever was needed, and the result of this is in your hands. It is an important contribution to the spiritual awakening of the people, to finding that "inner being" for which man has searched for centuries.

Robert P. Hutchins
Marin County

A WORD TO THE READER

Language is born out of tradition and carries a strong bias of the culture. When anything new is to be shown, when something that is beyond the experience of words and language is to be presented, words become a hindrance in expressing the meaning and communicating the feeling. Therefore, one has to depend more on one's awareness and intelligence to capture the spirit behind the statements, rather than get hooked on the traditional meaning of the word. Mind tries to comprehend the truth and aesthetic states through words, but words always fail miserably to give the experience of the state.

For example, the word "meditation" will never be able to give the reader the understanding of that state which the word signifies. To understand what the writer has to say about "meditation," "attention into oneself," "intelligence," "being in the present," or "being without thought," etc., the reader will have to come close to the author by leaving his own traditional stand. He will have to be open to capture the essence of the statement through unbiased attention.

Truth is not understood through words, and wisdom is not experienced through ideas and logic. Any deep understanding is the result of innate silence. Such silence lies beyond the frontiers of thoughts and words. Can a reader go through the words of this book with silence in himself, without the reaction of his traditional mind? Can he look beyond the sentence to gather the sense and essence of the statement? Can the reader be free from the rigidity of the word and dogmatic assertion of mind to feel the meaning that the writer is trying to convey? It is worth a try.

Through books and their reading alone, one will never come upon the state of creative silence where the experience takes place. Reading gradually becomes an intellectual game. The more one reads, the more he starts living in his exclusive idea world of time and less in total living experience of now. This book, too, can be a hindrance in coming upon that now wherein understanding happens.

One of the purposes of this book is to show the limitations as well as the futility of reading and of depending upon words and ideas to experience the truth. The moment this book creates such a hindrance and becomes a catch to the mind, the reader should be alert and attentive within himself, and be ready to throw this book out of the window, to be free from reading all such books from there on.

Dada

ABOUT THE AUTHOR

Who is he who can teach us about liberation? How does he know?
What university did he attend? From where does this knowledge originate?
Why is he talking with people? Where does this person come from?

       His family name was Dattaram M. Gavand.
       He is called DADA which means elder brother.
       He was born in Bombay, India, in 1917 September.

In his early years of family life
    He achieved
        Distinction in sports and photography.
        Success in business and social popularity.
        Material accumulations, comforts of family.

But seeing the limitations and futility of that way of life
    He gave up
        His family and business ties.
        His inheritance and usual identity.
        His opportunities for marriage and a comfortable lifestyle.

In order to devote his whole heart and energy toward finding the secret of life
    He faced
        Solitude and the challenge of the unknown.
        A life of austerity and misunderstanding from friends.
        Possible illness and fear of death.

In voluntary solitude and in communion with nature and life itself
    He understood
        How the mind works with its deceptions.
        How one destroys one's own happiness.
        How the mind itself is the burden and the bondage.

While in solitude, in an unknown moment of aloneness, suddenly
    He experienced
        The mystical explosion in his inner domain.
        The sudden flow of timeless energy within.
        A new state of ecstasy never known before.

The riddle was solved and the battle won
    As he discovered
        Peace and new order in life.
        A flow of creative energy.
        The mystery and deeper significance of living.

Having found in himself the song of life
    DADA now
        Shares with those who are eager to listen.
        Assists people to discover inner intelligence.
        Shows the way toward spiritual revolution.

Freedom From Time

Life has gathered Dust on the Way
During Her Centuries of Travelling Time.
Particles of the Dust
Have Developed into a Mountain
Which calls Itself 'I' ~ The Mind.

This Dusty Mold
Of Millions of Yesterdays Past
Is an Imposition and
Burden upon Life Energy.
Freedom from this
Dusty Mountain of Past
Is the Purification and
Liberation of Life.

Life Fulfills Itself
Through Its Own
Liberation.

Dada
Pacific Palisades ~ 1976

The Seeker

The Way

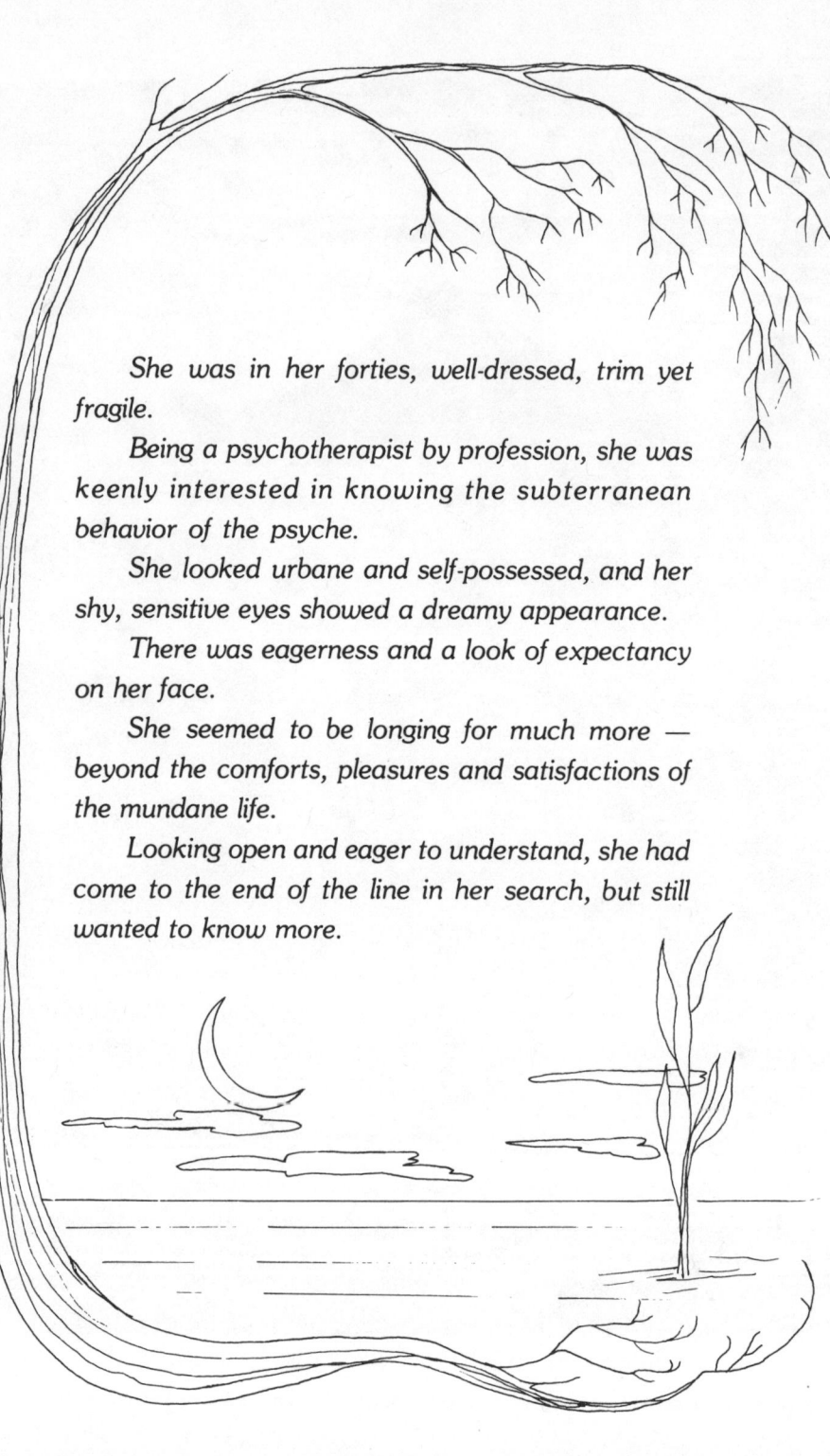

She was in her forties, well-dressed, trim yet fragile.

Being a psychotherapist by profession, she was keenly interested in knowing the subterranean behavior of the psyche.

She looked urbane and self-possessed, and her shy, sensitive eyes showed a dreamy appearance.

There was eagerness and a look of expectancy on her face.

She seemed to be longing for much more — beyond the comforts, pleasures and satisfactions of the mundane life.

Looking open and eager to understand, she had come to the end of the line in her search, but still wanted to know more.

1

THE SEEKER

What is the way of attaining liberation?
How can I live and work in the spirit?
Who will show me the path?

NANCY: I do not know to what degree I have made any movement in my spiritual development. I have been to the Holy Land and also visited the East, and have had many teachers and practiced many paths. Now I do not feel I know where I am going. I would like you to show me the right path. As a psychotherapist I earn enough money for my living, and try to use the other time to study and search more to find myself.

DADA: What would you do if you did not have the problem of earning your livelihood? If that were not the compulsion, what would you do with your life? How would you live your life?

NANCY: What would I do now if I needed no money? I would search inside and continue to understand the inner spirit. I would just live with the spirit.

DADA: (Laughs) Everybody likes to live with the spirit. But what is that living with the spirit? Can we live with the spirit?

NANCY: We do.

6   Beyond the Mind

DADA: In what way? How? Do we know the spirit? Do we know that quality which is the spirit?
NANCY: Yes and no. We have little glimpses.
DADA: Yes, little glimpses. But mostly what are you?
NANCY: Mostly what are we?
DADA: Yes. We may have glimpses here and there of that quality, but mostly we are only minds. We are living largely with our mind, isn't that right? We think about the spirit. We would like to live with the spirit. We dream about it, aspire to it, but we hardly know what that quality is, what that spirit is.

    Mostly the spirit is a part of our own imagination. Isn't that so? A part of the mind projects the images for which the other part is searching. It has the capacity to create the illusion of an experience through projecting these images. This is how the mind very cleverly plays with itself. So how are you going to discover that spirit so that you will have a direct experience of it?
NANCY: I want to know. Does your way of life do it?
DADA: Let us find out if it is possible to discover the spirit in oneself.
NANCY: (Pleadingly) Tell me how. How can I start to discover the spirit?
DADA: There is nothing like a positive start that the mind can make toward the discovery of the spirit.

> You start when you begin to see within yourself the constant pursuits of various desires, fears and hopes.
>
> You start when you become conscious of these subtle desires working all the time without stopping.
>
> You start when you see how your actions are the reactions of a biased and wishful mind, and that there is never a fresh action from life within.
>
> You start when you realize how you spend your entire life energy trying to fulfill the unending ambitions of the mind in all directions.
>
> You start when you recognize that you are never

reaching a point where you remain fulfilled.
You start when you see that you never attain these imaginary goals created by the mind.
You start when you discover that you do not really know what you want in life beyond food, shelter and a few necessities.
You start when you see that the mind is not interested in peace, but only in its own pursuits.
You start when you perceive and recognize that this mind is nothing but the burden of bygone memories.
You start when you see and understand clearly how this so-called mind is an imposition of unfulfilled experiences of the past.
You make a real clean start when you begin to watch every incoming thought and understand how the past is trying to continue at the cost of the present, calling itself "I."

Discovery of the deceptions of I, the mind, is the beginning of a journey toward the spirit.

NANCY: My mind sees this at times, but it does not stop there. It goes on building greater expectations.

DADA: Exactly! There is no end to this mechanical process of the mind. From childhood we are trained to expect more, to strive for more, and this mind keeps on chasing desires one after another until the end of life. Maybe this mind is just a mechansim, a habitual prison. We do not care to know what mind is; we blindly accept it. It may be only a crazy momentum, so do not take anything for granted. Desires come, thoughts come, and you are thrown into external actions. This ceaseless activity goes on trying to fulfill these thoughts. There is no ending to this constant thought movement, even during your sleep.

What is this all about? Each person has his own pattern of thoughts and desires; each one acts exclusively according to his own mold and conditioning. In this pattern of desires, we never can meet another person because we are so caught up in our own thoughts. There is no quietude in the mind, and therefore no room to meet anyone. Only when this mind is quiet and roomy, without desire, is there a possibility of meeting anything, even a flower.

NANCY: How do we quiet the mind and get rid of desire?

DADA: First, you have to see your constant false activity and understand these mad movements. Understanding quietens all of that. Look into yourself calmly, with sharp attention. To see what is happening in oneself is important. Watch every idea and desire that comes into the mind. Such observation is the beginning of quieting down this activity. Then you discover that you can look at yourself without any motive or expectation. Usually the mind immediately starts to name, describe, moralize and compare whatever it sees. But through unmotivated and unbiased looking within, you can step out of the field of thought. Just keep watching, and you will discover a new quality of sensitivity which is not a thought activity because there are no desires, motives, hopes or fears involved in that watchfulness.

NANCY: How do I keep that up?

DADA: You will have to discover that by yourself. There is no theory. You have to make a beginning somewhere. Be conscious of the thoughts coming again and again. See that it is so, that is all. This attention becomes a new vital point, an impersonal flow of energy. Mind is a personalized and conditioned energy. You have to discover the unbiased and unconditioned energy.

Proceed quietly, and then you will discover what meditation is. Attention without thought is meditation. Slowly through watchful attention you step out of the field of mind without any struggle. As your sensitivity increases, you will be able to act without the promptings of thought and desire. As you discover freedom from thought, you will be in the present — in the now — to act. This is not an intellectual process; it is something that you have to sense and experience.

NANCY: I cannot conceive of watching without my mind.

DADA: Of course not; our consciousness is not familiar with this kind of watchfulness. The nervous system is not trained to do this. The brain cells are not accustomed to looking back on themselves. The real challenge of life is to change one's dimension. It is not a matter of just altering a few habits or thoughts here and there. I am only concerned with the radical change, which is the discovery of a new consciousness.

We have to see how the mind itself is working and causing problems. We have to discover a sane and pure consciousness that can give us peace, quietude and happiness, and not merely indulge in thought/desire activity. The discovery of something much more fundamental is very important. Therefore, work with all your understanding, senses and whole energy, and not with thought/desire activity alone.

Now, how do we begin to bring about an end to this exclusive and biased mechanical thought process? Start from where you are, and begin by simply watching this activity. See what it is all about. Just watch. This watchfulness will bring about a quietude and will slow down this thought current. Then you will not be carried away so easily. The intensity of the watchful attention diminishes the flight of ideas.

NANCY: If I was without judgment, thought, desire and bias, would that bring about a discontinuance of all thoughts?

DADA: It is not so easy and automatic. As you move along, this watchfulness will broaden and intensify, gathering all the energy that the mind is now using. The more energy you will have for this watchfulness, the less there will be for thought activity. See the beauty of gathering this energy in watchfulness and attention without a thought. Then that energy will move on its own.

But the mind never sees this; it is always caught up in some problem. Then by the end of life we will be just "boiling the soup." We live according to the ambitions of our mind, wanting others to cooperate, but even if they do cooperate, it does not help. Our mind is a great manufacturing center of desires. Until we understand that fact and work our way out of it, there will be no end to desire and sorrow. Through desires we cause suffering for ourselves and inflict it on others. Then we blame them, even our loved ones, never understanding the cause and source of our conflict.

Survey your life fully to understand the beauty of it. When you understand yourself, you understand all of life. Only through this understanding is energy liberated from the domination of the mind. In this liberation lies peace.

Take the challenge which life has given you to understand. Perhaps some suffering is necessary to bring about this understanding. Therefore do not be disheartened by these difficulties; see the purpose in each situation. Be intelligent and come out of this stagnation into a new opening. See and experience the wholeness of life, and do not choose just through desire. Choose not to discriminate between good and bad, but see the whole structure of the mind which creates these labels. Then you will be watching your own tendencies without blaming others.

NANCY: I have to watch the working of my own mind. It seems so obvious, but I would never have come up with that, with my mind revolving around itself. I needed you to show it to me.

DADA: Perhaps my mission is to make people aware of themselves. This seeing and knowing one's mind is not book-knowledge or an intellectual process. This type of understanding will expand and intensify, and you will be able to know everything about life through your own internal attention, which is intelligence. This new gate of understanding will not be opened through ideas and concepts, because the idea can never give the experience. See the difference between idea and experience. We are constantly living through concepts and imaginations. Understand the fallacy of this conceptual process which prevents us from experiencing.

The state of love is not a concept. Mind can create an idea about love, but it will never experience the quality, the state of love. We must be free from this idea activity in order to have that experience of love; then your heart will open. Let your mind merge into the heart. It is the heart that will know. Then your life will be guided by love, affection, consideration and abundant empathy for everyone around. This is the real way of the spirit. Then you will love not only your husband and children but everyone. All the right actions will follow from that state of love. This is the expression of innate intelligence, which is the way to live in the heart.

NANCY: I can see clearly now what you mean by the spirit and its expression in daily life. Can anyone help find the spirit?

DADA: You mentioned that you have been to many holy lands of the East and West. You met several religious teachers during your search. What have you really found? Have you found the way? Now do you know how to proceed to discover what we call the spirit — that consciousness which is the spark of divinity? No one can help you from outside, as you alone have the means within yourself to discover and experience that quality.

NANCY: It comes to me sometimes, but I don't know how and when it does. I meditate and search in my own way. Sometimes it is closer than at other times. Often it is not close at all. Sometimes it just comes, and it is so beautiful, a wonderful experience, but I do not know how to have it come.

DADA: Yes. What is your process of meditation? How do you meditate?

NANCY: I relax, become quiet, close my eyes and just listen and turn upward. Sometimes I ask questions. Sometimes I express yearnings, like prayer. I try to wait, listen and expect to reach the spirit.

DADA: Do you do any chanting?

NANCY: I was given the mantra "Om namah Shivaya." Sometimes I do deep breathing. But mostly I begin to get very still, quiet and open. It is a habit, so I just open up to the inner self.

DADA: How long have you been practicing?

NANCY: About three years.

DADA: How far have you progressed?

NANCY: I try — I am not very good at it — but I try to bring the spirit into daily living with my family and my work. I try to have the spirit with me.

DADA: Who is that thing which tries to have? Tell me, who? Who wants that? Who is trying to have that spirit work?

NANCY: I am afraid, is it the mind?

DADA: The mind, yes. And so you shall never have it!

And what is this mind? Now let us go a little deeper into it to find out who wants this and for what. Why is this mind expecting these things, and can this expectant mind which is craving and aspiring for the spirit ever get it? As long as the mind is desiring the spirit, it shall never have it. So let the mind be quiet. This is not its business. On the contrary, this desiring mind has to come to an end.

NANCY: Even the desire for the spirit?

DADA: Yes, even the desire for the spirit. Perhaps this desire for it may be a blockage to the spirit. As long as the mind is active, nothing sublime can come in. The mind has to see its own fallacy of desiring, and come to an end.

One has to see what the problem is. The problem is the mind. It is ambitious and craves for so much. It wants things from the material world. And now it wants something from the spiritual world, too. It is aspiring all the time. It is the same mind that is busy in the material world now trying to find fulfillment in the spiritual world. There is nothing great about it, nothing really sacrosanct about the mind desiring the spirit. It is the same mind only desiring for something else now. And it is always the tendency of this mechanism to want more and more of everything.

So we have to question this very mind. Why is it desiring? Is it not happy with all that it has? Mind has collected so many things, but it is not happy; it is not content. It is never peaceful with those accumulations. As long as the desire remains unfulfilled, the mind just aspires and craves for it. And when the mind gets the thing it wanted, it immediately changes to new objects of desire. This movement of the mind is in the same pattern and moves this way perpetually. Through this pattern the mind keeps on craving and never reaches its fulfillment. It is the craving that we have to see and understand now. Why is the mind craving for so many things, even for the spirit? Why?

NANCY: That is what the mind is?

DADA: Yes, this very mechanism of craving is the mind. We have developed this mechanism since childhood. We want to catch things, to grab. The moment we are born, the first catch is the mother's breast to find food. The mind begins to acquire, possess and grab things, like toys and other objects. Then the psychological catches begin — my mother, my family, my home, etc. Later we go through school. We compete and want to win for ourselves. Everything becomes "mine, mine, mine!" This "mine" attitude keeps on growing with the passage of time. After that we want marriage and sex. Then we go after business, money and social prestige. By this time money becomes a catch — wanting a house, furniture, a car and so many other things.

After acquiring all those possessions, the craving for the spiritual comes in. It is the same desireful mind now aspiring for spiritual wealth. We listen to some spiritual talks, read a few books, and come across the ideas of bliss, nirvana, peace, happiness and so on, and the mind gets intoxicated, "Oh, let me have something of that world also!"

You must see that the basic tendency of the mind is to crave for more and more. If it is merely a craving for more, then the mind is not likely to meet that energy which we call the spirit. Mind shall never be able to grab that. *The spirit cannot come into the mental machine.*

NANCY: Then how can it come? What is the way out of this dilemma?

DADA: Is there a way? Put this question to yourself. If the mind cannot catch it, how can we have the experience of that quality which is the spirit, the soul, divinity? We never ask this question quietly into ourselves. We are always going after something or someone in the hope of finding the spirit from outside.

NANCY: Then should I ask myself?

DADA: Yes. No one will be able to give this to you. You can go to the four corners of the earth in search of holy lands; you can visit mountains and rivers, temples and churches, but nowhere will you find that spirit. It is not outside anywhere. This is not a gift or donation from anyone. You alone have to discover this into yourself. That is the only way.

When you see and understand this, you will have to come

back into yourself, not searching for it outside. All that searching is a projection of the mind through its desires and ambitions. This way your energy is thrown out in the pursuit of finding the spirit outside. All these drives must come to an end by your seeing the futility of this outer search, which is an illusive movement of the mind. It is just doing this through habit, because the whole mechanism is geared to looking outward. Mind is nothing but an extraverted activity. The pursuit of outer fulfillment is the objective of the ego at the cost of the energy.

This kind of thought activity will never find that divine quality, which is to be experienced within. It has its root only inside. So we have to come within to collect all that thought energy. By turning back toward its root, this energy is going to undergo a complete change. That dimensional change will give us the experience of a new energy, which is the flow of divinity.

NANCY: So it is necessary to stop thinking and doing a lot of other activities that the mind plans and pursues?

DADA: Yes, all this projected activity must come to an end because it is a waste of time and energy. For this kind of search and penetration, you will have to stop this energy dissipation and fall back upon yourself to keep it within.

NANCY: I understand; you mean gather it.

DADA: Exactly. The accumulation and gathering of energy to build a reservoir within is exceedingly important.

NANCY: Yes, yes. I realize what you mean!

DADA: This inbuilt reservoir of energy becomes a very vital and potent force.

NANCY: Oh, I see. I see! You do it by gathering the energy and not scattering it. It is clear to me now.

DADA: Yes, we must not scatter it. That is what is happening in the pattern of daily living. We are scattering our energy through thoughts and desires of the mind. We are also desiring this very inner quality through thought. So we have to see this energy dissipation and drop it.

Let thought remain quiet and not get concerned about it. Let that energy come back into yourself. Then it is going to show you something beautiful. You will immediately experience a new quietude, a silence within, because you will not be spending energy outwardly. It is the thought activity that is disquietude, whereas the negation of it is quietude and peace. So only when we fall back upon ourselves and gather all the energy within shall we know what peace is. In that peaceful moment you will be able to discover something sublime and spiritual.

NANCY: Oh, now I see the way.

DADA: So we have to work with ourselves and go directly to that core, to that center, to that root wherein lies the whole secret and mystery of life. You need not depend upon anyone, or on any book, in fact not on anything that is outside. Just be quiet into yourself. There will not be any thought to imagine or demand a thing. Simply be quiet with the total fund of energy within, and in such quietude you are going to discover something new. You will then experience what humility is, and what innocence is. The mind which is quiet into itself is innocent, humble, transparent and open to discover that which is the real.

Then you will know what meditation is. Meditation is not the chanting or singing of devotional songs, nor the repetition of any word or phrase. You will then be in a state of total surrender, alone within yourself.

You have to be really alone and anonymous to be with the inner spirit. When you are somebody, you are related to the world; you belong to the world. And as long as you are of the world, you cannot move toward the inner spirit; you will have no relationship with it. So to have a contact with the spirit, you will have to be alone, on your own. Then you will get a helping hand from within. The whole secret is to come back into yourself by gathering all your energy, and to be there in quietude and silence. To be in silence is to be near one's own inner spirit.

To be in such silence within is the highest form of prayer. Prayer is not chanting or singing praises to someone, nor asking and begging for rewards of the other world. Desires and supplication of thought on any level are not prayers. The silence of one's own total energy in the inner domain is the true state of prayer. Such prayer finds its own reward in a very mysterious way. The innate energy, when it regains its balance and stillness, finds its own fulfillment.

NANCY: Oh, I see now that what we call prayer is desiring. I have never realized that before. Now I can feel the truth as well as the strength of real prayer.

DADA: Yes, desire on any level is just a desire. The quietude which we are pondering over is of a different dimension. It is not a dull or docile activity but a vibrant state of inner being. That quietude is in itself very active and dynamic because it is a momentum of the whole energy.

When you make a focus of your energy by gathering it, it becomes potent. In that potency, thought, which is the product of lower vibrations, cannot operate. Then you will see all your desires as mere fanciful, lazy activities of mind and thought. You will know the difference between the two levels. The free and dynamic flow of inner energy is the real pulse of life.

So it is possible to come back into oneself to be in that moment of the present. But the present is hindered by thought that imagines the future and creates time. In fact, time is an illusion created by the imagination to escape from the present.

There is a constant movement of the present, a vibrant now which moves from second to second. The secret of living lies in the discovery of this now. Then you will truly be living, without imagining or hoping about the future, as there is nothing like a psychological tomorrow. You will be free from the future as well as from the past. Then you will have discovered the flow of the eternal now. This is the throb of reality and the momentum of eternity. It is possible to experience this momentum of now, and to live in it with each moment like a twinkling star pulsating with the fullness of life energy.

NANCY: Is it easy?

DADA: Sure it is. You have only to eliminate, through understanding, this imaginative and desirous mind.

NANCY: So you don't need the imagination?

DADA: No, not at all. Imagination is the fancy of the mind. It is an idea, the negation of reality. Why have imaginations about anything? Why not face facts as they are and let reality take its own course. Then you will have discovered a new way of living which will be your own.

Can you at least see the logic of this? See the element of imagination involved in the intellectual process, and be free of it. With this freedom you will be able to come back into yourself with all of your energy. This total energy functions through its own intuitive intelligence and allows no room for any imaginations of the mind.

NANCY: But I use my imagination so much. It has been of great value to me.

DADA: Yes, I know. But imagination has its utility only on the intellectual level. It is a hindrance in experiencing the spirit. So the problem is our own faculty of imagination, which is mind activity.

NANCY: So the spirit cannot be imagined. In reality it is beyond that.

DADA: Yes, you can never have it through imagination. Let the imaginative process of the mind come to an end. It is only in quietude that you realize the inner spirit. So the whole secret is here — to realize the quietude first. When you see the falsity of this mind game, you will drop it and not get carried away by it. The negation of this activity will bring about the quietude.

Disquietude is nothing but ceaseless thought activity. We try to quieten one thought with another idea, which then becomes a fight between two opposing thoughts. This way we remain in the same field of mind. This creates seeking, which is nothing but a struggle and conflict. We may hang on to some words, pictures, mantras, but again it is an idea, a seeking of the mind. Mind will never lead us to quietude. We start chanting mechanically, and again it becomes a habit of the mind. So we are never free from thought. The spirit is a quality of a new dimension, and thought has to resign for the spirit to come in.

NANCY: And that is not too difficult?

DADA: Yes, that is not too difficult at all. You have to see the fallacy of this thought activity, which is not the way to the spirit. The thought process blocks the incoming of the spirit. Not seeing this fact clearly, and ignorance about oneself, are the difficulties in realizing the spirit.

This perception is the way to understanding and self-realization. You see how the self is working, how the mind is functioning, and how thought itself is creating all these hindrances. Through self-knowledge you will be able to discover that quality which lies beyond thought. Since it is of a different dimension, the lower dimension of thought must come to an end. Unfortunately, we keep the mind constantly active trying to catch the other dimension through it. This shall never happen.

NANCY: It is not the right way. I can see now that it is an ignorance to use thought to capture that which lies beyond thought.

DADA: Sure it is ignorance. This is the whole secret of spiritual life, to understand the inadequacy of the mind — the thought — and to be free from it.

So the intellect has to come to an end. Seeing this whole game of desires, cravings, fears, fanciful imaginations and wandering thoughts, very quietly and silently within, is the way of meditation. Just watch it very impersonally. That impersonal watchfulness into yourself is going to generate a new quality, a new sensitivity, which will not be of the mind.

NANCY: Does meditation happen in silence?

DADA: Yes. Only in the silence which comes out of understanding.

(There is a long pause. The indescribable beauty of that silence is experienced. The quiet is interrupted only by a bird call.)

NANCY: (Obviously much more calm and relaxed, breathes a long deep sigh.) Oh, that is a big relief!

DADA: Yes. Whenever you see the truth, you get that relief. That is the action of truth. It is ignorance that binds, and the truth that liberates.

NANCY: (Happily) Yes! Free!

DADA: So it is possible to bring about a total relief and relaxation. And in that state the mind will never create a problem or friction. We are not interested in temporary relaxations, but in solving the psychological tensions once and for all. Then you will be at peace with yourself. You have to discover that state of existence in which there will be no problems. To bring about this dimensional change is the challenge of life.

NANCY: I did not really see it clearly before as a new dimension, as something separate, an entirely different quality.

DADA: The very quality of that energy is different, and we need that new energy for our existence.

Therefore we are interested in discovering that timeless quality which flows in the present. Through that eternal now you will discover a new momentum of life twinkling in the inner domain. Total conversion of life alone will solve the problems of the human being. Thought itself is incapable of solving its own problems. Only the higher energies can do this.

Spiritual understanding is the discovery of a new life energy which you call divine. Give it any name, but it is a quality of a different dimension. We have to discover that life energy, and for that discovery we have to bring about a total conversion in our psychological makeup. This is a revolutionary challenge which alone brings about a total change. So we cannot play with this psyche; that avoids the revolution.

NANCY: Yes, but we do play with it.

DADA: Yes, you do. I am not interested in this self-indulgent play. You have played with it enough. You have to take this challenge of your mind now. How can you take this challenge and go beyond? You have to be very, very alert and aware of all the thought activity. Only through this watchfulness will you be able to know the mind completely, inside out.

NANCY: Oh, I see. The mind cannot know itself.

DADA: No. It may imagine about itself, but it cannot know.

NANCY: But the watchful attention can witness and know.

DADA: Yes! Yes! The more attentive you are, the more you will be able to understand the mind. You will be able to see it very clearly. The mind is constantly catching you and making you act according to its own moods, sentiments and idiosyncracies. Your life is nothing but all this activity. You can capture the movements of your mind through watchful attention.

Then it won't be able to deceive you or catch you unaware.

NANCY: I have been trying to do an impossibility — use the mind to understand the mind.

DADA: That is the greatest illusion of life. Now it is time for you to see this fallacy. You have been deceived all the time through the mind. It is the mind that wants to know God, to know the spirit. But now we must be able to tell it: "That is not your business, dear mind. It is simply not your business. You are incapable of understanding and contacting the spirit. You had better be quiet."

The quietude that comes after realizing the limitations and ignorance of the mind begins to show the symptoms of a new intelligence. This inner silence is not enforced by the will. It is the outcome of deep insight and understanding the realities of life. Therefore, this silence is intelligent and eloquent. And out of this silence of inner space emerges the whisper of truth through an intuitive flash.

Silence is a state of aloneness, which is absolute. It is a state of surrender to life, the unknown. To face the unknown is to be free from all the reactions of the known, which is the mind. In facing the unknown, the energy becomes pure and sensitive to capture the new wavelength that flashes from beyond the frontiers of mind.

When energy becomes sensitive, highly volatile and effervescent, it transcends the idea/emotion level of the mind. Mind becomes the mindless. This mindless energy is dynamic, virtuous and holy. It is pure and transparent to reflect the will and glory of the divine. With humility the energy becomes capable of meeting every moment and event of relationship intuitively, without the thought process of mind.

This sensitive and humble energy becomes free from all ideas, desires and rigid mechanical drives born out of the past. The cumulative effect of the whole past is the image of "I," the mind which seeks the spirit. Elimination of this past is the freedom from mind, who is the seeker. *Thereafter all seeking comes to an end, as the seeker himself is dissolved.* Living becomes the experiencing of the total moment. With the discovery of living in the fullness of the moment, time merges into the timeless, and past as well as future are eliminated.

To discover this eternal moment, and to live in it anonymously, is the beginning and the end of all human search. This mysterious moment of the present becomes real and unending. Moment is the gateway to enter into the kingdom of eternity. Moment is the beginning and the end of all creation. Life fulfills itself through meeting the moment.

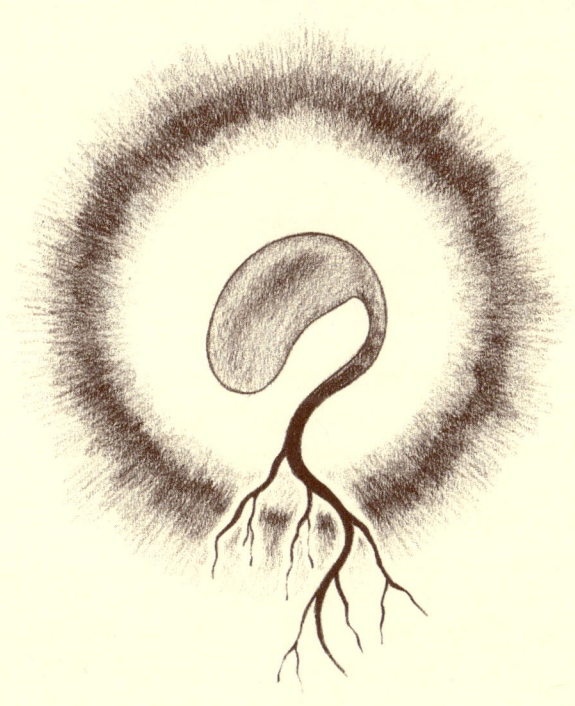

The Family Man

The Play

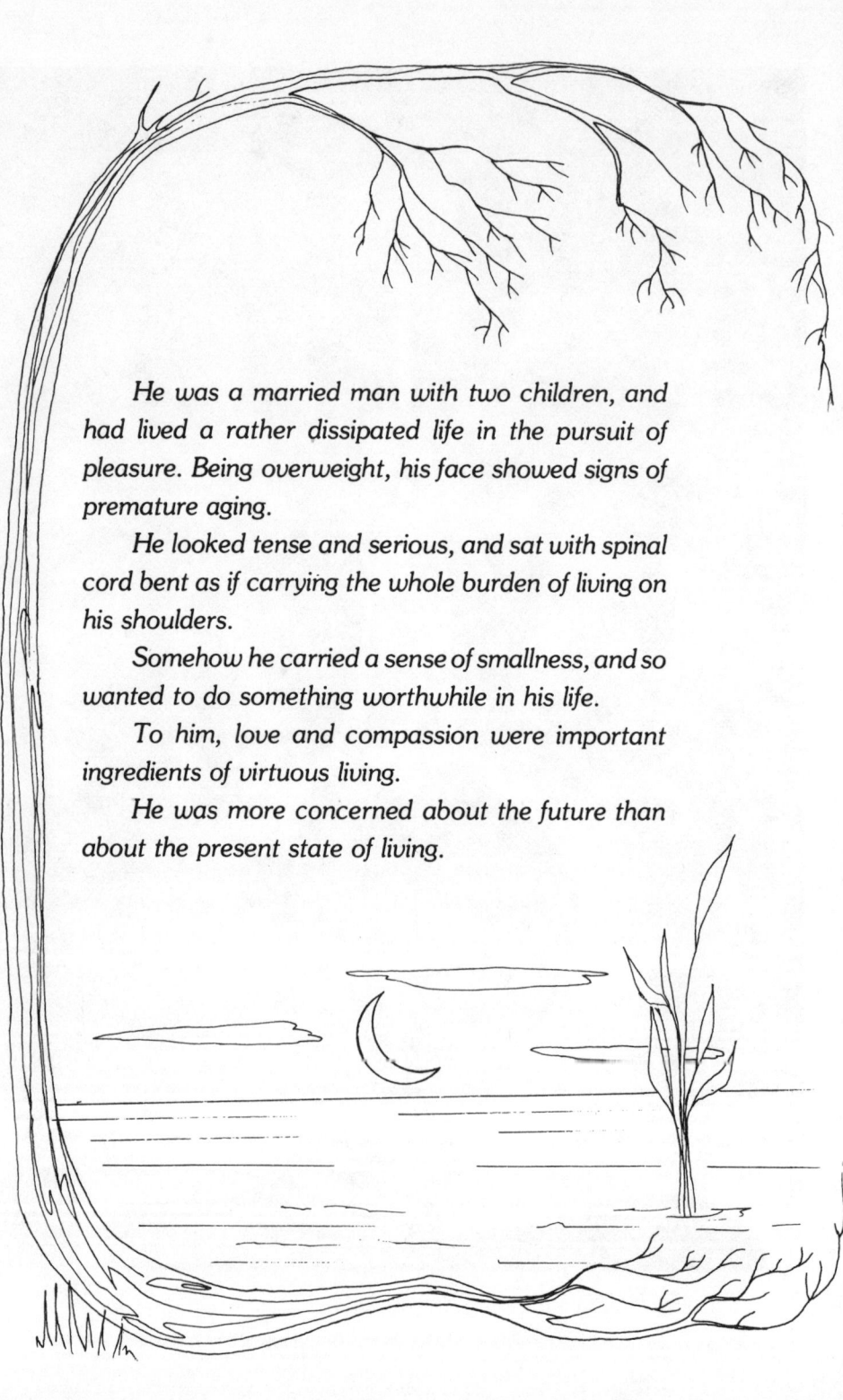

He was a married man with two children, and had lived a rather dissipated life in the pursuit of pleasure. Being overweight, his face showed signs of premature aging.

He looked tense and serious, and sat with spinal cord bent as if carrying the whole burden of living on his shoulders.

Somehow he carried a sense of smallness, and so wanted to do something worthwhile in his life.

To him, love and compassion were important ingredients of virtuous living.

He was more concerned about the future than about the present state of living.

2

THE
FAMILY MAN

What is love?
How can I love my relatives and friends?
How should a family man approach sex?
Has sex any higher purpose and significance in life?

MR. JOHN: Somehow I am not able to maintain relationships with my friends and relatives very harmoniously. I like to experience love with my wife. In fact, I would like to base my relationships on love with everybody around me. But in actuality it does not work. I am at a loss to know why.

DADA: How can we experience right relationship based on love? Who is it that experiences this love? What quality or element is this in you that is interested in relationship?

Can the mind experience right relationship? Can the thought process love another? Can an idea encompass brotherhood with all? We have ideas about loving, about brotherliness, but can those ideas ever feel and experience deep relationship? Can the mind understand this true love, or is there a different quality necessary?

Our mind expects affection and love, desires relationship

and brotherhood, and does at times experience a natural feeling of goodness. We might wish to treat everyone with brotherly consideration, but somehow we cannot do this.

MR. JOHN: Is that something which never happens, or just to a few people?

DADA: In rare moments we reach this experience, but once or twice in a lifetime is not enough. We must discover that state of pure love. The mind desires to have that state, but it is just a desire, an idea, which is imagination.

Everyone has this problem. The world is suffering from a lack of true relationship. People want to love, but cannot. The father wants to love the child, but cannot. The son wants to love the parent, but somehow there is friction.

Even husband and wife stay together for a few years and then start having some kind of friction. Why is it that couples cannot stay together very long, maybe two or three years, and then there is a breaking up? What happens even with goodhearted people? What is the missing link? Many couples live under one roof but hardly talk with each other. They live together only because they are afraid of loneliness and separation. Can we discover the right quality of attitude which will establish true relationship? Although people have some form of affection, they cannot establish right relationship through it. Friction arises. People try to improve, to better themselves, but it does not work. People with good intentions live on hopes for years and years, but still miss the real quality of a warm and deep relationship.

MR JOHN: I don't understand. Is it not possible to reach this love?

DADA: It is possible, but most often we just desire love, and it remains only a desire. The desires of the mind prevent that experience. Perhaps we are wanting too much and too many things in life. Mind is constantly occupied. Maybe when it is completely quiet, expecting nothing, a new quality will arise. But we are all the time caught up in the mind, with desires, ambitions, plans and expectations. Even for religious experience, it is the mind which is always hoping that prevents any spiritual realization. To have any spiritual experience, the mind has to become quiet and die down completely.

All thought processes must be eliminated totally. Only when the mind is quiet, when all the energy is at ease, then in that quietude something happens. But are we ever in that state? Are we ever in quietude? The mind is always busy, agitated. Even in the name of God we are projecting ourselves outward. These projections of the ego must come to an end. We project outward toward a person, a book or a picture, expecting something from them. There is nothing like a spiritual experience outside. We are always looking outside for something to happen, for someone to give us something.

When we begin watching all of these ego projections, all of the flights of the mind, and noting and being alert within ourselves, a new sensitivity arises. This new state of alertness is meditation. Then all of our hankering and looking outward comes to an end, and total silence occurs within. The whole energy gathers there; nothing is divided, and one is loyal to the inner energy.

Divided loyalties arise due to the mind. The beggarly mind does not know this inner fullness and devotion because it is always wanting something outside. Therefore, it creates the external loyalties and strives to go after them with the hope of fulfilling them in time. *Loyalty is a state of being, a faithfulness to the energy within.*

MR. JOHN: And does this new state of being come about spontaneously and without any method?

DADA: Yes, there is no method for the mind to arrive at this state of being. The state of fullness within oneself cannot be reached through any technique based on thought. The very activity of mind and thought is the denial of that state. This state of silence, which is fullness, is the negation of the thought process.

MR. JOHN: And once the understanding is there, the quietness comes?

DADA: Only in silence does understanding come.

MR. JOHN: Does internal help come from the intellect or from the heart?

DADA: All of this is imagining, as if the mind could know this. Don't depend on anything, not even on your own ideas or mind. Just be watchful and take nothing for granted, not even yourself. The mind is very self-centered and deceptive.

MR. JOHN: Can the mind be trained?

DADA: You can train the mind in any way you like. But that training becomes the mold and starts working mechanically. Such a mind will not know what the intelligence of life is. This trained mind will be efficient and clever, but it will not know what love and affection are. Training the mind is not essential, but freedom from all training, from all disciplines and regimentation, is essential. Freedom from all psychological contamination is necessary to build up a virtuous state.

MR. JOHN: When one does experience this dimension of the inner self, does the mind notice and become more cooperative?

DADA: No. When that experience is there, the mind is absent.

MR. JOHN: Who is experiencing the experience?

DADA: Energy which is free from the thought/idea/mind complex experiences the experience. The mind can never have this experience, but can only have desires, cravings and imaginations about it. The mind has to see its inability and simply die down. Only free energy is capable of experiencing. Mind throws this energy outward. When this wastage stops, the whole energy becomes pure and clean from thoughts and passions. The real secret lies in gathering the energy.

MR. JOHN: One of the energies I worry about is sexual energy, and I cannot go beyond it until I learn to use it in a mundane way. Sex is a strong drive. Effortful celibacy does not seem to work. I am interested in how a family man can handle it?

DADA: Somehow we have divided all this energy into different forms and have given them different names — emotional energy, intellectual energy, sexual energy and so on. I doubt that they are different energies; only our mind divides it into different patterns and categories. Life is one whole energy, and there is nothing like sexual energy exclusively.

The sex drive is strong. Trying to be celibate often leads to failure. When one is caught up in the excitement and sensation of the desire for sex, certain cerebral and physiological effects do take place. At that point the sex act becomes inevitable. There is obviously no escape.

But if one is attentive and watchful of the mind, to locate and see in oneself the buildup of the thought and desire for sex, one can slow down the desire. Desire is nothing but the movement of exclusive thought. When any one thought predominates and becomes exclusive, it becomes powerful. Such an exclusive thought affects the sex glands and the nerves, and excites the body. Then it becomes a psychosomatic demand. Tension builds up and release becomes necessary.

Anger, jealousy and fear are other examples of exclusive thoughts which build up strong impulses and affect the body and mind. So, there are various thought patterns playing within oneself which stimulate different actions. But basically all the effects are caused and guided by thought. Watch and see how thought arises and stimulates imaginations. Then you will be able to dissolve the sexual thought right at its beginning. We just have not been aware of the birth of thought, and therefore do not catch it. When you do catch it — perceive it at its inception — it is slowed down and finally transformed. The basis of sex resides in the mechanical character of the thought process.

To catch the sexual thought at its birth, before it arouses the mechanical process of the nervous system, it is necessary that we come back into our own center. We never take this journey into our own self. All the time we are extraverting ourselves.

Come back into yourself, and then you need not do a thing. With alertness and understanding there is no need for discipline. This watchful intelligence is not a mental process. In the quietude of the center, balance is present. This balanced energy acts intuitively from the spiritual level. You can dissolve all the problems of the mind and emotions by dissolving thought itself. In doing this you become free from the compulsive action of thought. This is the whole secret of life. Instead we go out to books, people, rituals, this and that, intoxicating the intellect. Can you take the challenge of a journey beyond the mind? Or will you just go on hoping, trying for a little change here and there in your thought patterns?

MR. JOHN: I know that many times my mind is crowded by unnecessary and mundane thought activities, and the thought of sex sprouts up mechanically. I can see now that with attention into myself I will be able to dissolve many such thoughts. But when a strong urge of passion develops, how can one handle the situation, especially when both of us are caught up in it?

DADA: When passion becomes strong and the sex act becomes an obsession of the mind, it creates a separation between the two partners. This kind of relationship between two separate partners, each one playing his own game with the exclusive drive of sensuous cravings, culminates in the sex act, which results ultimately in the loss of energy and in exhaustion. But the union of two polar energies, as man and woman, without any will of thought or craving of the mind, is a state of vital peace and love. This is the healthy state of love which rejuvenates and flowers up into humanness.

In the total merging of togetherness, which is the state of mindlessness, both can transcend sex and float in sensitivity, which is the prana energy. In this play of energy there is not much room for ego activity. The self is submerged in the flow of sensitivity, and a unique feeling of oneness is generated. This experience is the result of a union where there is no drive of the mind of any sort, conscious or unconscious.

Such a relationship between a man and woman is energizing and useful, conducive to compassion, love and understanding of each other. Herein is the marriage or the merging of two energies. The communion of two polar energies without the indulgence of thought is the state of marriage. *Marriage is a harmonious mingling of two vital forces, and is the state of mindlessness which is love.*

But the mind has the tendency to take a coarse attitude. This psychosomatic pursuit of carnal excitement stimulates sex and causes the relationship to degenerate into lustful activity, which culminates in the loss of vital fluid. Herein is the loss of energy, which is the invitation to exhaustion and the perpetuation of desire. This verily invites the end of the state of communion and love.

So if there is no desire and no drive of the aggressiveness of thought, nor any hurry to reach the end of the relationship act through orgasm, the union of man and woman can be an act of sensitive companionship. The total relationship of the whole energy between partners generates compassion and love for each other.

When the intimate love relationship between man and woman merges into one single act, the duality ends in one harmonious communion, and the circle of vital force becomes complete. This is a state of intense internal alertness in which the energy is released from deeper and stagnant pockets of the mind. One has to experience this total state of inner sensitivity without the agency of thought/desire/mind. This active, effervescent energy without ego brings about a unique quality of integration and togetherness. In such a meeting a new dimension of tenderness and compassion is experienced. Herein the ego loses all its assertive drives, and transforms into sensitive energy. A new experience of mindlessness begins to unfold. In this mindlessness and togetherness of two human beings a new beauty of relationship is discovered. This communion of two energies is the state of pure love. In that harmonious communion nothing is lost. On the contrary, each partner vitalizes the other. One assists the other pole to complete the circuit of vital force. This vital force rejuvenates both persons.

MR. JOHN: Is there any spiritual significance in living together as a couple? Can the sex relationship in the life of a family man like me help to enrich myself in any way?

DADA: With right understanding and meditative approach couples can transcend the mundane relationship of carnal and sensuous excitement into an enriching spiritual existence. The discovery of such a relationship between partners becomes meaningful. Then there is no usage of each other. There is no dominance of one over the other and no sense of inequality at all. A very intimate sense of oneness is generated. Herein lies the possibility of discovering the state of mindlessness and companionship which is the state of love.

In the right relationship with a partner, there is an opportunity of discovering and experiencing the moment of now. The sensitivity which comes into existence through the relationship of man and woman has the potential of giving the experience of nowness. In that state the whole energy and consciousness stay in the present. When approached rightly, one can bring about the contact of the now — the touch of the present.

With the drowning of the "I" in the flood of sensitivity, two persons can unite as one unit of energy, to experience oneness and establish communion. One can approach this communion consciously and allow it to happen with attention and alertness into oneself. The state of now is a rich experience. Then you become capable of capturing this experience of mindlessness when walking on a beach at sundown, or even while playing with your child. This way you can begin to move in the state of now in your daily life.

One need not depend on and indulge in the communion and mindlessness which happens at the moment of orgasm, which is involuntary. The voluntary or conscious approach to mindlessness is possible through understanding and experiencing the deeper sensitivity which generates through the relationship of a man and a woman. By floating in the flood of sensitivity, one can let go of the mind. One can feel and be sensitivity itself. Herein lies the opportunity to erase the mind for some time and to have the experience of mindlessness, which is the state of now.

MR. JOHN. Do you see much of this change going on?

DADA: I see much interest, but not any basic change. How are we going to bring about this change? It has to happen in oneself, and that too, right now. It is not a matter of believing this or following that, as we generally do in life. It is very easy for the mind to follow something. Through following, it hopes to change sometime in the future. Such hope is a deception. This way the mind has fooled us and will go on fooling us eternally. The mind cannot deliver us.

MR. JOHN: As I am talking with you, I can see how my mind is work-

The Family Man

ing automatically. It has become almost a machine.

DADA: Yes, an automatic machine, because we are not alert and watchful. Let your sensitivity function, and be aware of the beauty of it. You have to walk your own way into yourself. That wisdom is only lying within. Discover that inner temple of divinity. All of this mind gossip must end. It is the mind that plays in the name of wisdom and God. But the mind itself is the negation of spiritual activity and understanding.

MR. JOHN: I notice that I am very uneasy about this.

DADA: The mind creates a resistance due to its own vested interest. This new awareness eliminates the mind. The mind only knows barking, not loving, and is interested in living for its own bones. We have to change the quality of that dog so that we can turn doghood into Godhood. It is the dog, the ego, that is resisting and testing your understanding. You have to go through that acid test of intelligence to overcome the last crisis as a human being.

The final challenge for a human being is he himself — the I! In this challenge lies the opportunity for a man to discover his hidden potential. *In losing himself, man stands to gain the greatest prize of life — freedom.* The freedom from time is the state of timelessness, which is the liberation of energy.

MR. JOHN: It feels like I have no choice but to do that.

DADA: Yes. I am glad you feel that, because this is how understanding works. When you see something very clearly, you have no choice; it is just so. Perception of truth leaves no choice! It is a crazy thing to have one's own likes and dislikes about life. Any fool can do this, but only a few honest and intelligent persons accept the wisdom of life without choice.

MR. JOHN: Choosing it the way it is.

DADA: Yes, so there is no option left, and you let that truth lead you on. This new energy will take charge of your life. This new quality is quiet, alert, sensitive, attentive, and aloof from all thoughts and desires. Surrender to this whole energy is not like surrendering to hopeful images of the mind. You surrender to your own inner being because you do not have desires and choices. That energy of the inner domain moves very swiftly and spontaneously. There is no "you" left. Let us prepare ourselves for this mystical happening within.

MR. JOHN: So this new awareness is compatible with anything we do in our lifetime, such as my relationship with my wife and our physical attraction to each other?

DADA: The physical attraction will still be there. But that would not be the exclusive consideration. You would handle the situation in a very different way, and not be guided by the excited cravings of the mind only. The sensitivity, which is the mindless energy, is going to act in its own intuitive way. Then the loving embrace of your wife would be of a different quality. The whole approach and substance would change! Tenderness, compassion and love would be the guiding factors and not the passionate, sensuous thought. Then this refining of love is so simple, for it is the mind that makes our problems.

We miss the fragrance of life because the mind indulges again and again in old patterns. We must understand the whole game of the mind before we can do anything about God. There is nothing like divinity where there is mind activity. Mind may sing and dance in the name of God, but it is still the same old mind perpetuating itself.

MR. JOHN: You have opened a new door.

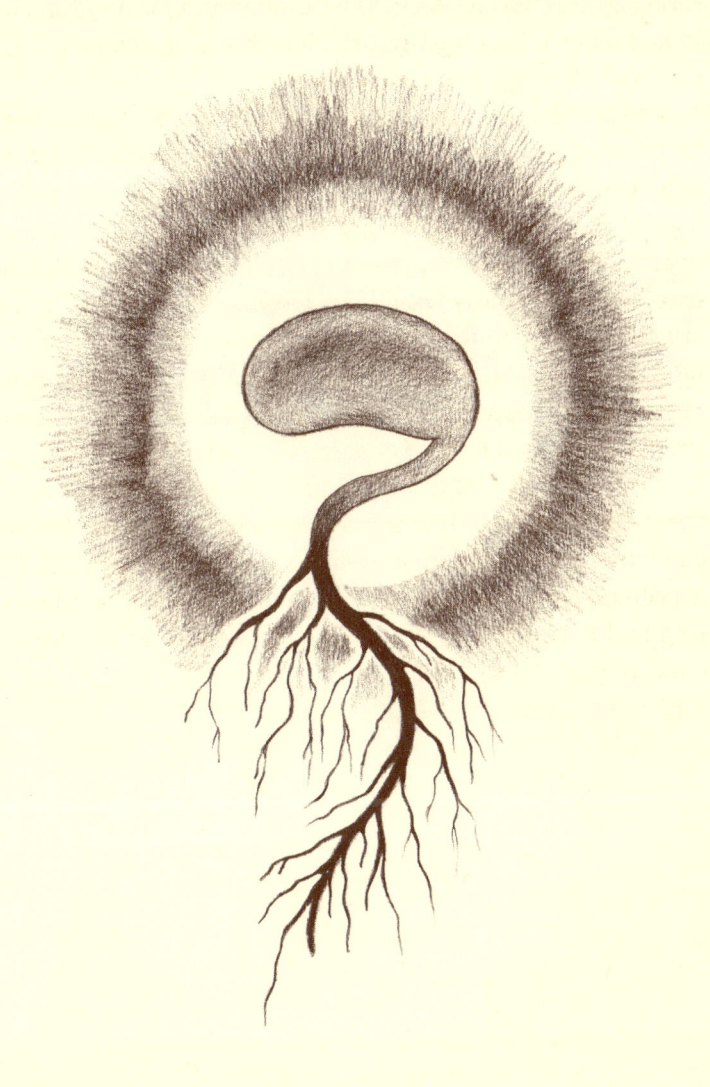

The Psychotherapist

Flowering

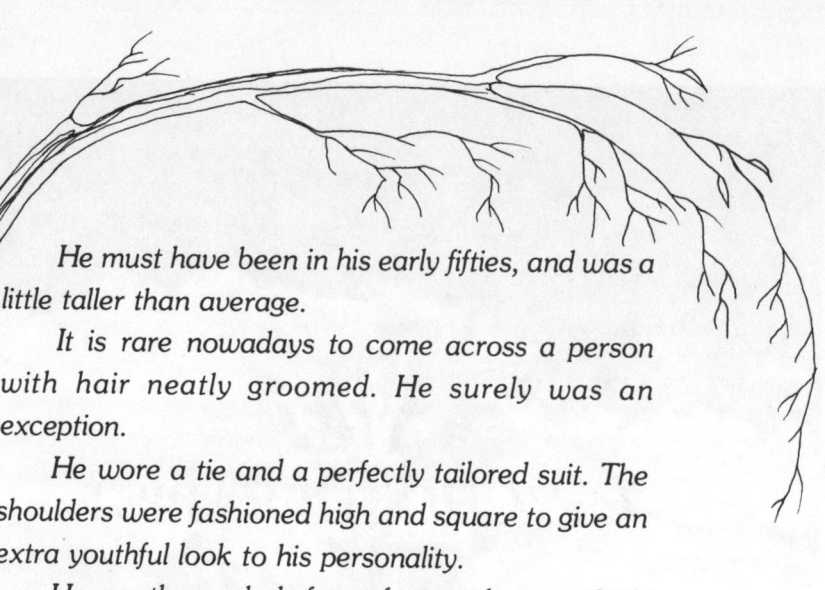

He must have been in his early fifties, and was a little taller than average.

It is rare nowadays to come across a person with hair neatly groomed. He surely was an exception.

He wore a tie and a perfectly tailored suit. The shoulders were fashioned high and square to give an extra youthful look to his personality.

He was the symbol of a perfect gentleman, which has become very rare in this "mod" land of California.

His face was square and carried a straight intellectual nose, and there was a scholarly look in his eyes. His eyes moved up and down quickly; they were sharp, alert and piercing.

With a smile he greeted me, yet the smile was not deep enough to have come out of his whole personality.

He looked well disciplined, as if he had been a perfectionist of long standing.

After taking a seat at a comfortable distance, he started talking in a low tone with a clear accent and calculated words.

His face looked more serene than the occasion demanded.

3

THE PSYCHOTHERAPIST

*How can I help others solve their
emotional and psychological problems?
What is healing?
Is it possible to change the mind?
How does spiritual understanding relate to daily problems?*

DADA: I suppose you are a psychiatrist.
DR. C: I am a psychologist and marriage counselor. I have been working with people with problems for about twenty years. I have also been working with meditation classes for about four years now and with spiritual groups. That is more and more my interest. Sometimes I don't quite know how to relate problems to the spiritual. That is something I am interested in, both for myself and for the people I work with.
DADA: So you are a professional psychotherapist, and you want to relate spiritual understanding, or spiritual energy, to daily problems?
DR. C: Right. These past two weeks I have felt a lot of inner direction coming to me. So I know that something is happening and that this is an important time in my life.

DADA: Do you practice meditation?
DR. C: Yes.
DADA: Daily?
DR. C: Yes, for about four years.
DADA: What type of meditation do you practice? To which group do you belong?
DR. C: I do not belong to any group. I have been a seeker, and have been to many groups and many teachers. There is no one method that I follow; it is more spontaneous. I want to increase my spiritual awareness and the inner connection. I have been going to many places and reading a lot of books, but now I feel I must trust the spirit more and turn inward. I feel I was directed to come here, that you could help me.
DADA: It is good you are working with your meditation. There is much interest in this country in meditational activity. People are searching for something, something they do not know. There is a yearning, an inquiring and pondering. But the people that I see here are scattered. They do not know exactly where they are, or what they want. So they generally catch on to anything that is foreign to them, unknown to them — that is what is happening.

The mind is so eager to find out that it becomes impatient and loses the sense of discrimination. One has to be very careful about this catching, this drifting. The mind is a very clever instrument that we have built up. It is always holding on to something and trying to achieve in time. The mind creates a hope and then goes after it in hopes of achieving something tomorrow. There is nothing like tomorrow. Tomorrow is a fiction, an idea, only a concept of the mind.

What is reality other than the present? *Now* is the reality, but we are never in the now. Mind is not interested in the now, as it takes its shape from memory, from the past, and thinks about tomorrow. The mind moves from the past to the future, hardly recognizing the present. The mind may think about the present, or have a concept of it, but to be in the present is different from thinking about it.

Mind, which is nothing but ideas and thoughts, is not

capable of being in the now. It is the now that negates thought. The present is a state of being. Idea or thought is a conceptual activity which works through imagination. To be in the present, imagination has to come to an end, which is the state of existing without thought.

DR. C: Are we thinking right now?

DADA: Is it a matter of thinking or just of being aware of oneself? Is there a thought process going on? I do not have any thought process. I am not working through memory. I am nowhere else but in the present.

DR. C: You can talk about the mind, but still be in the present?

DADA: Yes. Words come, but the whole state is in the present. Only then can you exist totally and completely with all of your energy. Thought is a partial activity, just one aspect of consciousness, a compartmental drive and not a total activity of the energy. Thought is a look through a hole. Ego is interested in just one aspect, and looks through that limited hole. Then another thought comes, and another — an abundance of thoughts and desires. One thought is active at one time, and another is active at another time; in this way the activity goes on perpetually. Each thought and desire works in a separate compartment, and we never work wholly with all of our energy. This is our problem. We do not work with a total perception of life, nor with a complete understanding and involvement; therefore, there is never a total action anywhere.

The secret of life is to bring about this totality of perception and action. In thought we are never a whole unit; we remain partial, exclusive, compartmentalized. This partial, exclusive activity creates our problems. When the whole energy is active, there is no problem. It sees everything completely, through and through, and action is also total. With such action there is no residue left in the mind. No memory is left behind. One can live without memory, without thought, when one exists in the present. *This whole energy in the now is the spirit of life, uncontaminated by thought or desire.* The spirit of life is free from exclusive ideas, free from memory and from time. This whole energy is a state of timelessness. You can discover this state right here, right now.

DR. C: I can feel it. It is like I am floating.

DADA: What you are experiencing is not thought, but a higher state of sensitivity. This quality of sensitivity will assist you to be free from all partial activity of the thought process and from all memory activity. It is important to gather this energy. In this state you can be free from your own self. There is no freedom other than this. We are bound by our mind, our memory and thoughts. Freedom from this bondage of self is the ultimate liberation. But as it is, our energy is being used by this partial activity of the thought/emotion complex. The mind is constantly using the whole energy for its own continuity and the perpetuation of its past as well as its future. Therefore, there is no freedom at all for the expression of our energy in the present.

DR. C: I want to discover more of this energy.

DADA: The mind is using this energy through its compartmental activity, and brings about conflict and friction within its own structure. Devoid of thought and mind, this energy is completely free.

DR. C: Are you saying that the mind binds energy?

DADA: The mind binds, divides and plays with it. The mind fragments this whole energy into intellectual, emotional and sexual energies; it prompts many drives, excitements and cravings. Energy itself is whole and it is complete, but the mind divides it, creating friction and conflict. We have to see this clever device of the mind. When you discover this total energy, there will be no room for thought. Such total energy without thought is very dynamic.

DR. C: Is the problem that we misuse the mind, or is the mind itself the problem?

DADA: Mind is just a thought process. *Where is the mind if there is no thought? Is there anything like a mind, or even you as a psychological entity, when there is no thought?*

DR. C: You are making words right now; are they thoughts?

DADA: Words are an expression of the whole energy. This energy activates me and moves my hand to touch yours. My touching

The Psychotherapist 43

you is a spontaneous expression; it is not an action of desire. In thought there is always a motive, a desire. In whole energy there is no motive, no thought; it is a continuous, spontaneous action which is intuitive and pure.

DR. C: You are expressing truth. You are not trying to influence anyone?

DADA: I have no ideology. I am not at all interested in influencing anyone. I will assist people so that they will perceive the truth in themselves. Mind complicates everything with motives, with many separate desires. We try to use the mind to solve the problems created by the mind! It is not going to solve them. Mind itself is the creator of all problems.

How many problems have you solved, and how many people have you really helped? You may solve one problem, but the same mind is going to create another one the next day. Mind is always doing this mischief. Can the mind ever solve these problems? In the process of finding the solution, it generates more and more conflicts. Let us be interested in the basic solution, otherwise we will be perpetuating more difficulties. Show people that this is so; show them the problem-maker. Help people to uproot this very problem-maker. That is the only solution and the only way.

This is why the whole world is full of confusion and conflict. With all of our so-called progress, education, affluence and scientific achievement, where are we? Is the man of today an ideal image of the human race on planet earth? He is mentally and emotionally fragmented, living in fear, conflict and suspicion. He creates barriers, frontiers, religious and racial groups, ideological and cultural separations, political and psychological exclusions. The interpersonal as well as international relationships of man are not the way they should be. I see so many people with affluence and education, but they are all filled with problems. People use drugs of all kinds and indulge in various escapes to try to relieve their worries and conflicts. This is only running away from the truth of the matter. We worry; we are burdened with conflicts. Where is our progress?

What is needed is a basic understanding of life. We need

to know how the mind is working and why it is constantly active. We must ask if it is the right kind of mechanism for us, or if it is just some crazy, uncontrolled machine. We have accepted this mechanism of the mind blindly. We know little if anything about how it works and why. We do not observe all the intricate activities of our own mind.

Through all of our life this mechanism keeps us active spinning ideas, spinning desires, and we never take a moment to look at it. There is no end to this desire activity, or to the pursuits and ambitions of the mind; there is never a fulfillment of it. The more we have, the more desires we generate. The rich are never fulfilled, are never satisfied and never arrive. Why? What is this craze of the mind which makes us unhappy and empty, which nothing fulfills? We must take a look into this mechanism, this structure we call ourselves, to know all of its workings from close quarters.

DR. C: How do we see the mind? Can we watch it rather than get caught up in it?

DADA: Usually we try to know and understand, but somehow we get caught up in the mind again. Even your meditations and so-called spiritual aspirations are the projections of the mind, and in this way it perpetuates itself. Anything which perpetuates this mental and intellectual process does not lead to the spirit or to divinity. This quality of wholeness is beyond the region of the self. This mind activity has to come to an end completely in order to take the journey beyond. We must first see the game of the mind, how it keeps us busy, engaging us all of the time, even in the name of the discovery of that which is beyond.

God is also an idea of the mind. Do we know what God is? Do we have any experience of Him, or is it just a creation of the imagination? We have read about Him; we have heard about Him; the mind has picked it up, and now it wants to have that God. But can this mind ever have God? Will it ever experience Him?

Before we take up any discipline or meditation, we have to see very clearly what is happening. Otherwise, we are very likely to get subtly caught up again in various desires and other mental activity. As long as this mind is busy with desire, pursuit and ambition, we will not be able to get out of the field of thought. Actually there are very few essential activities of the mind. Most of the activities are false ambitions springing from attachments and imaginations. The sublime, the spiritual, lies beyond the field of the mind. We have to see clearly and be free from this mental activity, or nothing spiritual can come in. The first step is to cut down all the activities which perpetuate the mind and intellect by seeing their falsity. But we do not see this clearly; therefore, we go on playing with it. That is why we read so much, to find answers through books. Perhaps you, too, may be reading books. Do you?

DR. C: Yes.

DADA: See how the intellect, the mind, tries to know and experience God through books. You must have already read many, and where are you with all that reading?

DR. C: In no way closer. Not very happy!

DADA: Yes. Then what is the use of all that game of the intellect? Can we ever find God through books, ideas and dry words? Divinity is a state to be experienced within. The pursuit of ideas must come to an end if we are to know Him. But thought and intellect, being external drives, hinder that experience. Mind can imagine about truth and God, but it cannot realize them. To experience this quality, one must free all the energy which is being used by thought activity. One must see the delusion of using thought to find God.

The first step then is to see this clever game of the mind which keeps us occupied all the time. How do we free this energy from the domination of thought? We do it by bringing this energy back into oneself and collecting it within. When it is free from this domination and sufficiently collected within, it acts in its own intuitive and mysterious way. Free energy is the pure stuff of life. When uncontaminated by thought, it leads to right action, because there will be no compulsive force of the mind behind that pure energy.

DR. C: Doesn't mind ever know the right action?

DADA: It just imagines that it does, through its own conditioning.

The mind uses and misuses energy, holding it outside. The whole process of spiritual activity is to see the limitation of the mind and free that energy from its authority.

DR. C: How do you know when you are in the mind or not?

DADA: You can see in your alert attention; you can feel it, without making any idea. You can see and sense the fragrance of your own freedom. Slowly you discover the process of freeing the energy.

DR. C: How do we free the energy?

DADA: We free our energy by seeing how it is bound by thought. See how thought grips this energy and enslaves it perpetually, making us arid and empty within. We must see this whole game of thought going on continually. We are one with the thoughts we think. Thought is I. The moment there is a thought, there follows an action. Are we ever conscious of this? Do we ever question this thought or look at it? When we do look at it, we can comprehend the illusive nature of thought. This attention into ourself is the beginning of understanding, which comes about through unbiased, unmotivated perception.

Do not get caught in doing anything about this thought activity — even in trying to change or amend the mind. Just perceive the mental activity as it is taking place without any desire or intention. This new perception — this attention and alert watchfulness — brings about a new sensitivity which is impersonal.

DR. C: You are not interested in changing the mind?

DADA: Not at all. You cannot do it. For centuries this game of changing the mind has been pursued. We can condition part of the mind, at a certain level, through morality, education and ideologies, but we cannot change the whole man. No nation has transformed man through its political systems, philosophies or constitutions. *Regimentation of the mind is not the true change of man.* I am not interested in altering the mind to make it a little better or broader, but in working to dissolve it, to bring about a new quality of consciousness which will act in its own way. Change is understanding, which is a total process. This new consciousness is of a higher dimension and will eliminate the whole mind game.

You cannot change the entire structure of the mind, even if you take years and years; it is so mammoth, so huge, and is hidden in different layers. You simply cannot change it. Some psychologists try to, by playing with dreams and teaching the technique of self-hypnosis. Other psychologists use reward and punishment methods to change attitudes and behavior. But are these techniques going to bring about a real revolution in man? These are all peripheral changes. *The need of our time is a basic change at the very center of man himself.* To be free from the mind, a new approach and a new sensitivity are required.

The mind is a leftover of past experiences. It is the inertia of the past which continues as memory. This dead inertia lives again at the cost of energy of the present. Beware of this game and leave it alone. Discover this free energy, the new momentum in the now, and be with it. Have nothing to do with the past, and then you are free from all the problems and the problem-maker itself. We need a basic dimensional change, and not just a few amendments here and there. This is the only way to solve the human predicament. When you are free from the problem of the past, then you can help others.

Step out of the prison of the mind. Leave that prison, and let the walls collapse. We must have a radical, revolutionary change and not just add a few new ideas. But instead we try to change the walls of that prison, to make those walls better, more modern and more decorative. For centuries it has been the same old stuff in new clothing. We need a dimensional change now — a total revolution within man. For this revolution to happen we must be clearly and alertly watchful into ourselves; this is the way of meditation.

Meditation is not a process of the mind or the ego on any level. Rather, it is an understanding of this clever, cunning activity of the mind. Meditation must be the way of life, not a part-time affair where you sit for half an hour. The way of awakening, which is meditation, is through a constant vigilance into yourself. When you are attentively watchful within, you will be able to realize and understand yourself. When you see the false activity of the ego, you will stop seeking. In this way of meditation you will accept life as it is, by totally meeting your surroundings. You can then wholeheartedly accept your wife as she is, without a thought of changing her. You will really love and sincerely care to be with her. But the mind is always expecting something else, wanting some change, only according to its own conditioning. In this mind activity, you never accept anything or anybody fully, even the wife whom you love. Total acceptance is the negation of mental conditioning, which is the way of meditation.

DR. C: Do you accept that the other person has the problem of the mind also?

DADA: Yes. The other person, too, has the same problem. But you have to take the initiative and make an opening from your side. The right attitude from you is going to influence the other party. Accept her fully and allow life energy to do the work. In total acceptance the mind has no activity left, and so you can dissolve it more easily. In acceptance you will be free from all reactions. Your state of non-reaction is going to affect and influence the mind of the other party. With your right attitude you will help the other person to find balance and moderation.

Mind which functions through reactions and carries the prejudices of the past is the cause of crises in relationship. It is full of conditioned reflexes which have established total control over life energy. There is no free energy available for any independent action or spontaneous expression. That is the poverty of our life. Yet we never realize it; we do not become conscious of it. All of our life is invested in creating and solving problems. The mind has no other business but that.

DR. C: Then there are really no problems?

DADA: Find out what the problems are, and see where the problem-maker is. If the mind is not, there is no problem-maker and there are no problems. Mind manufactures them through its desires and imaginations. It tries to control the energy completely through all of its motives, pursuits and imaginary moves. All of this movement ends when you accept life as it is and embrace it with an open heart. But now, because of the constant activity of the mind, there is no room for the heart. The dominating authority of the mind is the problem. We are constantly working with our heads, allowing no time for the heart. We talk about heart, we imagine about it, but we are never in that state of being. It is the opening of the heart that will accept everything. In that acceptance the mind becomes quiet, and the tranquil energy begins to function, which is love. And this way of love is to live in the spirit.

The spirit functions and has its own spontaneous action without the thinking process. He who lives in spirit becomes simple, humble and whole. In this wholeness of energy there is no room for thought.

DR. C: The thought of money and the pursuit of it are very strong drives of my mind.

DADA: We surely have to have money, but there is a limit. We need money for survival and existence; it definitely is a need. But one should be watchful to find where need ends and greed begins. Mind, being a mechanism of continuity and perpetuation, often begins with need and ends with greed. See everything in right proportion. Discriminate. Otherwise, the intoxicated mind drives you on and on, all the time money, money, money. It becomes a burden on life with its excitements and obsessions.

We need right understanding about all activities, not only to solve problems, but to discover a state of innate happiness, peace and joy. All these qualities are outside the field of the mind. We have to be free from the clutches of the mind to discover this new dimension of life — this real wealth. You will then be full with riches. Life will shower its riches upon you in abundance. Then money will not be a craving of the mind.

DR. C: I understand that the discovery of this new-dimensional energy is the real wealth of life. I would like to search for it. Do you think much energy is misused in spiritual searching?

DADA: Much of this spiritual searching is just another pursuit of the mind. Instead of material pursuit, we start on a so-called spiritual pursuit which subtly becomes another activity of the mind. Be cautious, be alert, and watch if the spiritual goal is only a mental process.

Through attention we discover a new quality of perception. It is not mental and involves no desire. There is no motive in this watchfulness. It is just an energy, a sensitivity, and it sees spontaneously. This attention — this perception and watchfulness — is a unique quality of energy through which you step out of the field of the mind. In this movement of energy, be careful that thought and desire do not enter. Watch the thought activity with no motive. Although such perception is foreign to the mind, just perceive.

This state of watchfulness is the beginning of right meditation. Discover the real state, not the self-perpetuating mental activity with all its rituals. Chanting and breathing are very easy activities; anyone can do them. They, too, can be another of the self-perpetuating tricks of the mind. It will not be enough to amend the mind by changing a few things here and there. The mind energy has to be basically altered. The mind is interested in changing thousands of things, and you are not going to achieve all of them anyway. We have played enough with the peripheral changes. See the futility of all such attempts. Be interested only in a revolution at the center.

DR. C: What is the best course of action when you find yourself in the middle of some mental activity?

DADA: Watch whatever the mind does; let it have its action. Then you will not be indulging because you are aware of it. The drive of the mind is so strong that the action will take place. Don't resist. Do it. Complete it, but be aware of all that; be attentive. Attention is more important than action. Act and finish up the thing, but keep up the watchfulness. Let the mind act, but be aware while it is acting. Watchfulness is understanding. See the whole game and watch it with mobile attention. Watchfulness is not a thought. There is a subtle difference.

Can we look at a rose with our whole energy, our whole attention, and without any expectation, desire or description? Can we see a sunset without thought? Can we be sensitive without any movement of thought and desire? With this sensitivity, any experience is full and complete. When one is totally accepting, there is no mind left to create a disturbance in the energy. Right action will come instantaneously. Such action does not come through desire or negation, but through acceptance. In total acceptance there is no mind trying to change anything. Action which comes out of such acceptance is creative, and often you are not aware of it. But still, the energy acts in the right direction. Then it is not a partial activity of thought but a total action of whole energy.

Life is not the continuity of the mind, but the creative momentum of pure energy. In this momentum, no residue remains. Only then is action full and complete. Whatever you do is enough. This new consciousness, this spirit, is always complete, total and active in the present. The present moves on from second to second.

DR. C: I feel completely out of the mind right now.

DADA: We can discover this mindless state which is meditation. We are meditating now. In this state there are no problems.

Humanity has to discover this new life energy. It is not just your need or mine; it is the need of the human race. *You can bring about this change in humanity only by bringing it about first in yourself.* One has to be faithful to the energy within, and then it will express itself in right action. Those who are capable and who have the capacity of understanding will bring about this fundamental change.

So, basically, we have to take the challenge of this mental activity. We have to displace this thought process through understanding, to go beyond it. We cannot eliminate it by resistance or suppression. Just look at it with watchful attention into yourself, which is understanding.

DR. C: Can we see our motivations this way?

DADA: Yes. Then we see the motives and origins of many thoughts. We will see this mechanical process. Most thoughts are superfluous and false — just fanciful imaginations. But when we are not watching them, we are yet engaged in extravagant mental activity. See all this and you will be free of it. Perception through total attention brings about freedom.

DR. C: Mind is motivated by fear, desire and ambitions?

DADA: Yes, and by so many other things. Fear, the sense of insecurity, and many of the desires and ambitions are mainly the outcome of our imagination.

DR. C: And the mind through this imagination has caused many human illnesses?

DADA: Yes, there are different types of sickness, but most of these are psychosomatic disorders, and very few are real illnesses. When you are free from this thought activity, and free from fear, the physical body becomes tension-free and functions automatically to regain its health.

DR. C: Is it not necessary to be concerned about one's health?

DADA: No. You need not be concerned at all. You will see that when there is proper balance within, your health is there. Disease is a state of lack of ease in the body and in the mind. When you are at ease, there is no disease.

DR. C: So, to be aware of the mind and to release its energy is healing.

DADA: Yes. That itself is healing. Then the whole energy works smoothly, in perfect balance. Disharmony is disease, and harmony of the whole energy is health.

DR. C: When the mind tries to be the director of life, everything gets out of order.

DADA: Surely. Not just a director, but let me use another word: *dictator*. With its great dictatorial authority, mind is using all the energy. Therefore, through watchful attention, which is understanding, we have to dethrone this dictator displace him and be free of him.

DR. C: Then there is no dictator left?

DADA: Yes. Then what is left is pure and free energy which acts through its own intelligence. That free energy is the intelligence of life. It knows its own action and its own direction. That is the state of liberation, and in that liberation lies the freedom of life.

(Silence for a few minutes)

DADA: Do you have any further questions?
DR. C: Before we conclude, I would like to focus on some specific questions with regard to how this spiritual understanding applies to my work and my patients. My main question is, what can the therapist appeal to in the patient for healing? What is this human potential that we speak about? In the therapy situation, is the healing element the attitude of the therapist or what?
DADA: Basically, healing has to come through one's own understanding — from within the patient himself. The wrong attitude and behavior bring about some kind of disorder and imbalance. To create balance, the patient must regain right understanding; then right action sets the whole thing straight. Healing or repairing is undoing the damage. The function of a therapist is to assist the patient to discover his deficiency, his imbalance, and then help him to regain that balance. When the mind is functioning better, it is much easier for the therapist to help him see the facts of his illness in right perspective. And this will give the patient the opportunity to repair himself.

The problem with a severely disturbed patient is that he is not in a balanced state of understanding. Helping such a patient to bring balance is often difficult and nearly impossible because his mind is not functioning normally. When it is so, such that he is unable to understand the language and logic of the therapist, then what other means are there to bring about the balance of the mind?
DR. C: In some cases we have to modify the environment of the patient so that the outside influences can be more normal, especially where there is stressful pressure and friction.
DADA: Yes, the environment plays its unique part in bringing about understanding — the right type of environment for the particular patient. Where there is a more congenial atmosphere, the patient can react less and gather more understanding. Involvement plays a part in bringing about understanding — the right type of involvement for each patient. When the patient is affected by fear, he should experience a different type of involvement in which he is not so affected. Indeed, he must have an

environment of abundant love, care and consideration so that he can be free from fear and return to normalcy.

Yet somehow these matters are incomplete. The patient may forget about the fear which he is carrying somewhere in his mind. A loving environment may assist this person to forget the real cause of the fear which is in his system. He may never be able to understand that cause, that symptom, and dissolve it. The new environment may enable him to forget the cause, the disease within, but then the new involvement becomes an escape for him. He will appear to come to normalcy, but will still carry the seed of fear within himself. Then the same problem is likely to arise again in relationship to another incident or person.

Basically, he will be sick within all the time, although he may forget about the seed of fear he carries. Deep down within he is always carrying this scar. That is how the human mind works. The conscious mind is influenced, guided and stimulated by such scars kept within the deeper layers of the mind.

So we need to have a real remedy. Otherwise, this is just like suppressing the symptoms as is done many times in modern medicine.

DR. C: Do you mean that even if we have a congenial environment, we still have to understand the cause?

DADA: Yes. Many modern drugs suppress all the symptoms, and the person feels he is healthy again, but these symptoms arise in some other way. That is how ill health grows within all the time. So, is it possible to repair the damage without throwing it underground, pushing it somewhere into the subterranean flow of consciousness?

To repair the damage in a patient, the therapist has to have a deep understanding of his own life, of his own mind and how it works. It is true that the therapist through his mind is going to help the patient. Only a healthy mind can affect the other mind. Assisting the patient is not an intellectual game.

When the patient has lost the capacity of understanding and the normal ability of thinking logically and sanely, the therapist has to provide that understanding through his own energy. By talking and being with the patient, the therapist has to affect the patient with his own life force. That is a very, very important means of bringing about a change in the patient. It is always the uncommitted energy that brings about a change. By uncommitted, I mean free. Only that quiet, silent energy which dwells within is capable of bringing about understanding. So, without contacting the mind, the idea level of the patient, the therapist may contact that life force behind the idea activity to bring about the right understanding.

DR. C: You mean the therapist cannot speak from one mind to another mind, but can speak from his energy to the other energy.

DADA: Exactly. This energy is the right instrument of healing. Healing can happen only at that level of energy. But generally a therapist tries to convince the patient by ideas, to establish a relationship on a verbal level alone. Talking may be the means, but that talking has to be the expression of the pure energy within; then it is going to affect the patient. He may not even understand the therapist or follow the logic of his talk, yet something is going to touch him. Some energy is going to contact him and help him establish that balance again.

So the real work of a therapist is to discover this energy within himself and work with it. *He alone is a healer who has that abundant energy to supply to the needy.* It is not through ideas and techniques, nor through convictions of the mind, but it is through the energy that healing takes place.

DR. C: It means the therapist has to know when he is in tune with and is functioning in his own energy in order to help the patient.

DADA: Yes, that is the way of helping the patient. Disease is an imbalance in the flow of energy. The hindrance in the free functioning of that energy is the cause of illness. So to bring about a balance, one has to work on the level of mindless energy. Then it is possible to bring about sanity and balance without touching the mind or the idea level. Basically this is the way of a healer.

DR. C: Is this energy the healing element in the human potential?

DADA: Yes, this pure energy, this elemental source of life is the human potential. This energy has the capacity to repair any

damage anywhere. The freedom of this energy is perfection.
DR. C: So the very presence of a centered therapist would be healing to the patient, whether he might use physical, mental or emotional techniques.
DADA: Whatever methods he might use, basically this energy is going to do the healing. Right involvement with the environment and various methods of treatment may take care of the outer form of the patient, but the real disease lies in the imbalance of this energy, in the blockage of energy. Only the centered therapist can affect that energy source in the patient. Right environment influences the patient to get some necessary relief, but this relief is not a cure at all. These so-called healing techniques and approaches are only environmental influences, which offer temporary relief to the patient.

Some medical doctors work with this elemental energy, which has the capacity even to diagnose a condition. From this elemental energy they can find out many things intuitively. Doctors of real genius are those who work with this kind of energy, which brings the cure. The true healer may work with his hands or with chemicals, but basically it is the energy that cures.

And so, finally, it is not science, techniques or theories that are important, even though they have some significance in this whole structure of curing the patient. But it is this vital energy, which is the creative force of life, that is important.
DR. C: There are many scientists and healers interested in the question of energy today. Energy seems to be the focal point in bringing together many sciences which have become separated by their own peculiar languages, methods and philosophies. The sciences were becoming so fragmented that there could not even be communication within the same field between the theoretical and applied specialties. But energy has become a bridge of contact within and between sciences, religions and philosophies.

For example, Wilhelm Reich was an early exponent of orgone energy as universal common denominator between science, medicine and psychology. Reich used breathing and other techniques to help move energy through blockages in the body. Reich was rejected during his lifetime, but now is finding much wider acceptance. Maybe he was working with physical and psychological energy. It seems that some kind of discrimination has to be made as to what sort of energy we are talking about. In all sciences, different kinds of energy are worked with and described. Now we hear a lot about psychic energy.

DADA: Yes, we do. But I am speaking of that elemental energy which lies at the source of all the expressions of life. There is one basic energy. All the others are compounds and mixtures, moving and working in different directions and on different levels. Scientists are not yet aware of this basic, elemental energy. They are playing with different expressions of it. These so-called energies, such as psychic, sexual and emotional, are not pure forms because they are affected, stimulated and diluted by the mind.

DR. C: I can feel the truth of what you are saying; I just feel it inside. There is a need for this pure energy.

DADA: This pure energy is the need of life. It is life itself.

DR. C: What you have said is touching. I really got a lot of insight from talking with you. But I feel that what is more important is the peace, tranquility and understanding which I have gained from being with you for the last hour. I feel I am experiencing what you mean about the therapist's energy level being the crucial factor in healing.

DADA: That is how the energy works; from one source it touches and affects another.

DR. C: You mean like your energy is touching me?

DADA: If it is working and active in me, it is bound to have its effect. This energy is the real life force. He alone lives who has discovered this basic vitality. All others just continue in time, with the impact of the dead past.

We have played enough with the thought/emotion energy. Now the human race has reached a stage where this mind is becoming a hindrance instead of a help in the upward march of life. Mind has turned this energy into a self-centered and stagnant momentum. Now those few who are capable and intelligent must come forward to take up this new challenge of change in the very center of man.

We need a few people who will be the pioneers of this new change. Humanity today is in desperate need of a total revolution in consciousness. Political and cultural revolutions bring about some partial and superficial changes, but they are not enough. We need a change in the very depth of man, which alone will bring a radical conversion with the sprouting of a new universal consciousness. We need a global man who will be a resident of this planet so that this earth will be our home.

This unbiased attention in the moment is going to take man beyond the frontiers of the mind, into the region of universal intelligence. This is the possibility right now. By converting this self-centered mind energy into the impersonal intelligence, man on earth stands poised today to reveal the beauty and mystery of new-dimensional existence.

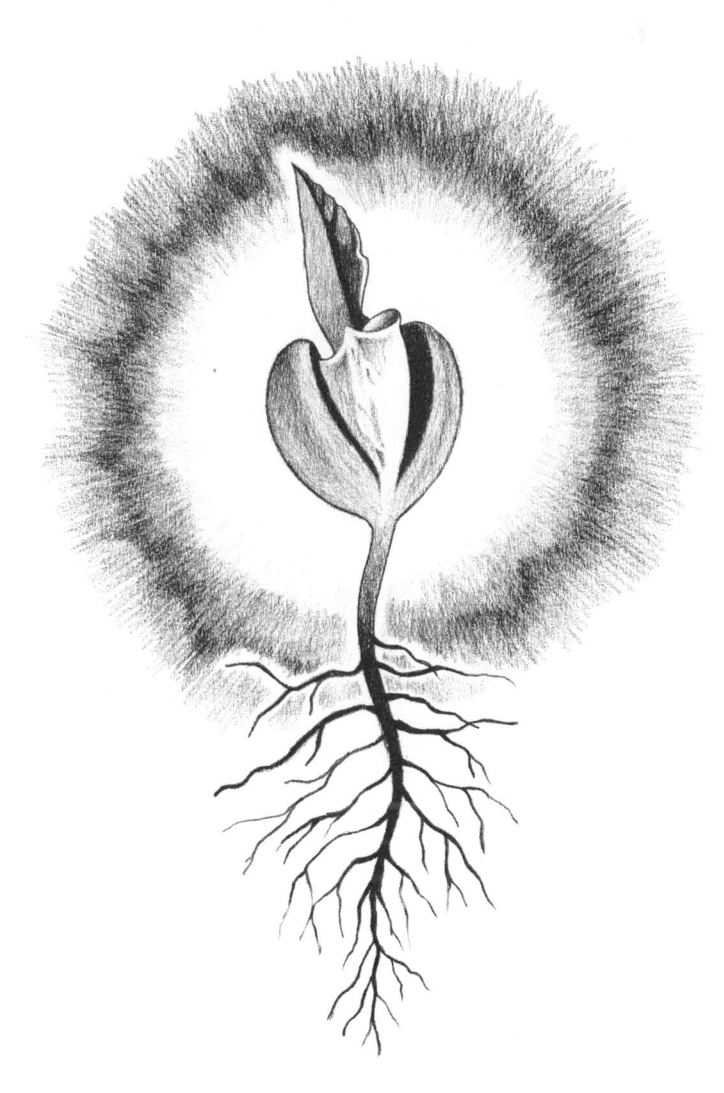

The Wealthy Person

Imprisonment

An elegant new red Mercedes came up silently to the porch and stopped. Out stepped a tall man moving in a sober and serene manner.

He walked into the house with an air of dignity and a strong sense of superiority.

There was an appearance of conservatism on his face, yet he was trying to be playful by twirling a key chain that he was carrying.

He appeared fresh-shaven, clean and smart, and the hairstyle looked perfect with his long hunting coat.

Along with him he brought some books to show me how many different teachers and philosophies he had investigated.

He had traveled extensively to visit almost all the religious people of his time and to hear their spiritual discourses.

He had read many books on religion and philosophy as well as gone through workshops on modern confrontation and relaxation techniques.

Yet he seemed more concerned about his health and wealth than about God.

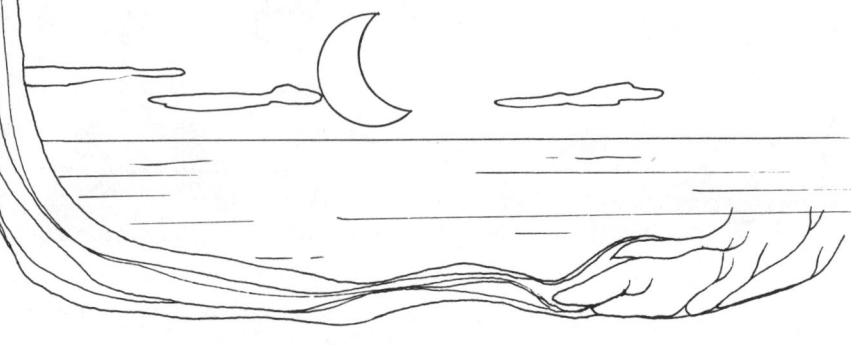

4

THE WEALTHY PERSON

Why does being rich prevent me from being happy?
Is wealth an impediment in attaining spiritual freedom?
Is there such a thing as peace of mind?

BOB: I inherited money from my family and have spent a good deal of my life and energy in the world of investments and finance. I find that my outlook and that of my friends toward me has been influenced by economic considerations. How can I understand life so that I am free from the distrust and tensions that money brings?

DADA: Economic status must not influence understanding of life. It has to be free from one's economic position. Yet we are constantly reacting outside to society in terms of this economic influence. Can we be free to realize life without any bias? To understand life one has to be free from the power of monetary status, reactions and resistances. Only when you are free from the negative or positive bias and prejudice of the mind born out of wealth will you be able to comprehend life as it is. Neither poverty nor prosperity should affect understanding, for the understanding of life springs from freedom, and has nothing to do with material wealth.

Yet we are not free from these influences and resistances. Is it ever possible to be free from our economic position, with its particular conditioning, to understand life as it is? In your case you have more wealth than you need, therefore your problem is that of a rich man. Should riches affect your understanding of life?

BOB: No, but it does.

DADA: Your wealth and philanthropic works do affect your relationships with family members and friends, and also affect your philosophy of life. Your lifestyle is conditioned by this wealth. Any kind of conditioning limits understanding.

BOB: It begins from being born into a wealthy family.

DADA: Yes, so you have a different set of problems, the problems of a rich environmental conditioning. Your richness is at the center of your mind all the time, and you are acting and reacting only from that position. Can you do away with all of these psychological impositions? Can you be free from the ego of wealth? It does not mean that you have to give up your money and become a poor man.

BOB: I may be rich today, but it is possible I could be poor tomorrow.

DADA: Poverty and richness fluctuate; they are just a social and economic status, having absolutely nothing to do with the understanding of life. Such understanding is quite an independent phenomenon, and we ourselves are never independent enough to see that because of the dominant influence of money on the mind.

BOB: How can I be free from the influence of economic status?

DADA: First, you must see how much it has affected your psyche and conditioned your mind, and how you tend to look at everything through that viewpoint. Your mind is conditioned by ideas of being born rich, having money and spending lavishly on your family and friends. These factors are always in the background, influencing your thinking and feelings and affecting your actions. When you decondition yourself, perhaps you will be able to look at life freely and impersonally. You have to

The Wealthy Person   65

work at being conscious of this conditioning. Otherwise, there will be no freedom of looking. Recognize how your entire thinking process is rooted in this status and this conditioning. See the harmful and limiting effects this conditioning has had upon your relationships and understanding. When you see in each action the harmful and limiting effects upon yourself, this clear perception itself will find the way out. Recognize also how your wealth has influenced your thinking about your relatives and friends. Riches are helpful, but your entire outlook is dominated by this factor. You are not really free to think, and therefore cannot have a real transparent friendship with anyone. Both consciously and subconsciously, money affects your perceptions about yourself and others.

We have to be conscious of our self, about what is happening to us, what is happening to this energy that we are using all the time. If it is affected by a physical illness or mental disturbance, the energy will not find its right action. Also, when this energy is influenced by either poverty or wealth, it is difficult to discover the intelligence of life. This energy should be pure and free so that it can act effectively and rightly. It has to be uninfluenced, well balanced and unconditioned, so that it will bring understanding to show you the truth of life. The freedom of that energy opens the way to understanding. When undominated by thought of any kind, the whole life energy becomes available to establish the right relationship with everything and everyone around.

BOB: But my mind is always busy with thoughts.

DADA: We are all the time in thought, whirling around knowingly and unknowingly, with all the background of the memory mind. The whole past is there, with its motives, ambitions, habits, jealousies, angers, neurotic blind spots and fears, working subtly on all levels. And we are never free from these thoughts. We never know the freedom of this whole energy. Therefore, we are never truly creative, living in the present; we are never in the now, in the spiritual moment. Something is dominating, something is pushing and pulling us all the time. This is a very poor way of living. To live with those pushes and pulls is the way of poverty. To live in the freedom of this energy is a creative and rich way of life.

Rich is not he who has many possessions and big property, but he who has freedom from craving. You have to discover that richness of life; you cannot inherit it. As long as one is not free from his conditioning and the domination of mental outlook, one cannot be truly creative, and will never know the richness of free sensitive energy. Only in that state of freedom from all cravings are you rich, full, complete, quiet, serene and tranquil in yourself. The real wealth of life is this freedom. Because you are not aspiring, not hoping, you can just be there, balanced and tranquil in your own complete energy. To be in the present is the richness and fullness of life. When you discover that quality of fullness, that state itself will show you how to live. Then you will not be prompted and guided by riches or by monetary considerations.

Now you have to see how your actions and reactions are influenced by that economic background. When you understand how you are being influenced, money will not be a catch. When you see and realize in every action how your whole energy is being consumed by this background of wealth, you will begin to be free from this conditioning.

BOB: I guess everyone has conditioning of some kind.

DADA: Yes, and conditioning of any sort is harmful. Poor people, too, have their own conditioning. Perhaps they envy and hate the rich, and develop some inferiority complex and fear of the future. Freedom from conditioning is the beginning of understanding. Yet we are not free from this influence, which prevents understanding. Understanding is an act of free energy. We must see how we lack this freedom of energy and how the whole personality is influenced. Everywhere and in all experiences of thought and emotion we are constantly being conditioned. We have ideas about everything, but we have no understanding. Ideas are imaginations about the future. We are never in the state of understanding, which is always and only in the present.

It is possible to miss being in the present throughout one's entire life. We may never feel the freshness and fragrance of the present. We may talk about the present — that state of spirituality — but are we ever in that state of the spirit? We always miss the present. To be in the present is to be one with the spirit. Spirit knows no past or future. It just functions in the now, which is eternal. The moment of now is the freedom from time; it is the movement and flow of eternity. It runs on and on from second to second. It works like a twinkling star. It just moves on and on in our inner space. The movement of now is the throb of eternity.

But unfortunately, we have hardly any experience with this quality because we are moving in the field of ideas.

BOB: How can we be free from all these thoughts, from all the influences of the mind, and bring about more energy?

DADA: When the whole being is there with total energy, there is nothing like a lack or an insufficiency of energy. Abundant energy is there. But we try to have more spiritual, physical and mental energy, as though there are separate levels or qualities of energy. Separate energies do not exist. In the mind we imagine that there are different kinds, but this is a fallacy. There is but one source of energy. With the discovery of this source, a fund of energy will be available, and then there will be no dirth.

Let us discover the fullness of being in the present, where this pure fund of energy exists. Then life becomes bountiful. Such an abundance of free energy is the fullness and richness of life. In this abundance there is no craving on any level of existence. Life then works very mysteriously. It fulfills itself. Life then moves on with its own momentum and works through its own intelligence. Such an intelligent momentum is the state of creativity, which is a state of fullness, happiness and ecstasy. *Rich is he who enjoys this state of fullness of his own inner being.* There the life energy is complete and in the now. How do we miss this present moment? We play with many things of the mind and of time. Mind stagnates and perpetuates itself by functioning through time. The mind guards itself so as to remain the same. We never experience in life that real fundamental change, that real conversion of consciousness at the center.

I am not interested in the approach of becoming a little better and a little more relaxed by playing around with all kinds of popular techniques. We are always trying to be a little better in the future, but we spend our whole life the same way. And where do we arrive at the end of life? We remain the same. What we need now is a complete change, a total revolution of consciousness. Yet we never work for that. We are content with a few little changes here and there. We settle for a little relaxation on the physical level and for a little more energy for the mind. For what — for more indulgence?

What is happening to those people who have a little more physical and mental energy? They become more clever, but what do they gain with this cleverness? Are they not using this energy for their own selfish pursuits, drives and ambitions? We know how clever people work in society. The problem is not how to have a little more energy, but how to understand the whole process of this energy. We never try to understand the significance and the intrinsic purpose of this elemental energy. We have enough energy, but how are we utilizing it? We crave for more, without seeing what it is. What are we doing with that energy we already have?

You have a good physique and good health; you have money, intelligence and capabilities. All of the assets of life are there already. How many people are so fortunate in the world? You were born in America, you live in California. Everything is so beautiful here. What more could you want? With all of these good things and blessings bestowed by nature, what are you doing? How are you using all these assets? Still your mind continues to hope, seek and desire something different from what is. What does this mind want now? Have you ever tried to find out? Is the mind ever really at ease? Is the mind happy with anything? Or is the very character of the mind to hope and run after something that is not?

The mind is always unhappy with what is, craving for something in the future. The mind does not know how to be in the now. The real poverty of the mind is its incapability of being in the present.

BOB: Why is it that the mind cannot be in the present?

DADA: The mind moves on and on because it just cannot be quiet. We do not really need anything else in order to be peaceful and free in the present, but the mind is always agitated and uneasy with itself. The mind cannot be silent to take a look and feel what is here in the now. With silence and attention, we can discover a new quality of wealth and warmth which is the state of the present. *But the mind cannot permit this looking.* The mind constantly craves, plans, imagines, aspires, chatters, and we call this our intelligent way of living!

We do not pay attention to that true quality of life, the life of freedom and quietude, the life in which you are truly creative and active within yourself. In this dimension you become sensitive, alert, dynamic and peaceful in the present. This is the activity of the whole man, of the whole energy in the present, whereas the action of an idea is always an exclusive one, through fragmented drives. The real action — the spiritual expression — comes out of the integration and total understanding of life. Although at first we begin with an intellectual perception, we must go beyond the intellect. See that there is nothing sacrosanct about this mind, these ideas and desires, not even about our mental activities concerning religion and philosophy. By seeing the falsity of the constant agitation of thought, and by dropping it, a new dimension arises. This new dimension is unconditioned, unfluenced and unmotivated. This new consciousness is not influenced by poverty or riches, but is independent and free.

BOB: This is what I want to understand more fully!

DADA: This freedom, this intelligence, is not the monopoly of any religion or of any country, East or West. Do not divide life into different factions and regions. Only the mind divides us. Clear perception is an act of universal intelligence and belongs to no one person or region exclusively. The whole world need this understanding without divisions. This dividing of life has impoverished us. The poverty of life is the constant pursuit and craving of mind. Mind is the beggar in oneself. *Even the rich man is a beggar, constantly craving after something.* There are beggars as well as super-beggars in society. *Rich is not he who has more, but he who longs for no more. Poor is not he who has less, but he who craves for more and more.* The discovery of this wealth of wholeness in man has to be the new religion of the world. If at all you give it a name, do not get caught in that name or turn it into a dogma. This is the new consciousness, without conditioning and without superficial divisions. When you are whole, this energy acts in its own intelligent way. Then you do not have to be concerned about the right action, because this energy, being the intelligence of life, will find its own action intuitively.

BOB: I am getting glimpses of this intelligence.

DADA: This intelligence works without conditioning, without imagination and without any thought process. The whole world needs this unbiased, impersonal and universal intelligence, which will bring about right action with no reactions. Such undersanding, which is the result of innate intelligence, can release us from the problems created by the mind. If we continue to follow only our conditioning and traditions, we may destroy our civilization. Our old attitudes will not help us now. Traditions, whether Eastern or Western, are mechanical processes which negate understanding. We cannot just accept these cultural values. We have to see from moment to moment and understand the whole significance of life. This intuitive intelligence does not come from traditions or books, but is innate, beyond all influences. Finding this, you will be free from your mind with all its conditionings. You will then have discovered your own guru in this fundamental intelligence. The totality of your energy, this basic innate intelligence, is your guide and guru. You are going to have your guru right within to lead you on toward the summit of life. The wholeness of energy is the liberation of life.

I am not interested in bringing about just a few external changes in man, or only in improving the mind. That is always going on. What we need is a basic revolution at the center of consciousness. For ages we have played around at the circumference. There is no end to making adjustments and improvements. In the new dimension, man will rise above himself to become a truly integrated human being. Man has the potential to become a superman.

BOB: We are really activists here in America, trying lots of different techniques.

DADA: The more active we are in the mind, the more clever and modern we think we are. Constant thought activity in the pursuit of ambition is the dominant trend in Western culture. Modern living is nothing but the unending pursuit of thoughts and desires with all their excitements and sensuous temptations.

Now we have to go beyond all cultures. We have to transcend time itself and discover that state of the timeless. This timeless is the pulse and momentum of the now. The whole secret and beauty of life lies in the now which moves on with its freshness in each moment. This fresh moment is full in itself and is untouched by time. Only in that timeless state will you be truly rich. Freedom from time will bring you the new riches of life. You will be rich and full there, without any possessions.

Life gives abundantly to him who drops, through understanding, all the possessions of mind. Energy dispossessed of everything is pure, free, aesthetic and divine. To be with this purity of energy and divinity is to be truly wealthy. He is the rich person who has discovered this hidden wealth of life.

The Researcher

Maze

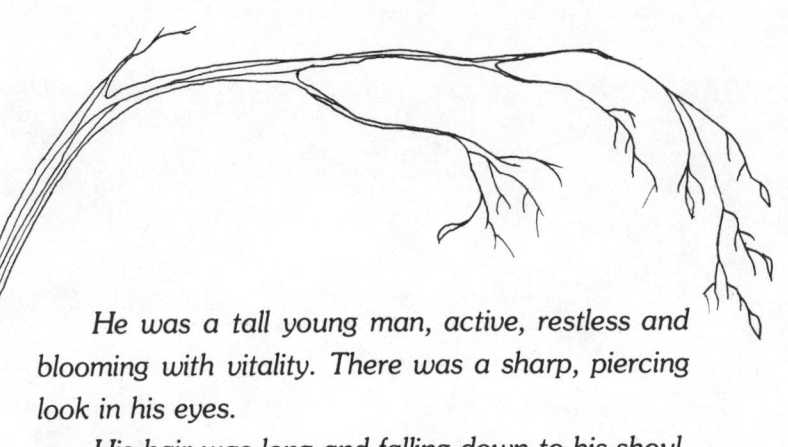

He was a tall young man, active, restless and blooming with vitality. There was a sharp, piercing look in his eyes.

His hair was long and falling down to his shoulders. It had a natural curl, and his hairstyle gave a certain yogic appearance to his face.

He wore an Indian-style kurta and Indian-made sandals, which lent a distinctively Eastern touch.

His nose was short and high, and in spite of his youthful years, there was a shadow of rigidity on his face.

There was a sternness and seriousness in his looks. He sat in front of me with his spinal cord straight.

His mind seemed very active, and there was determination on his face.

His personality appeared obsessed with something.

Perhaps he wanted to make his mark on life.

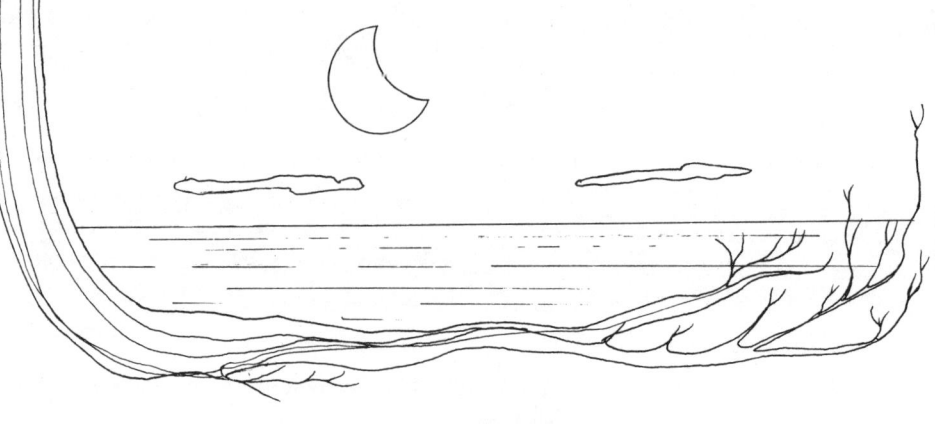

5

THE RESEARCHER

Is it not a fact that through scientific research and conclusions we can educate and change the world? Don't we need more information to convince people? Would you cooperate in measuring your spiritual energy in the laboratory?

DR. R: I have just returned from India, where I received very clear instructions on the performance of yoga asanas and pranayama. I am teaching yoga classes now, and I am interested in doing research on yoga.

DADA: You must be practicing yoga exercises daily and very regularly.

DR. R: I try.

DADA: Try? (Laughter) After learning yoga and teaching it to others, don't you feel the necessity of doing it for yourself?

DR. R: Yes, I do. I practice at least five minutes daily, although I should do an hour and fifteen minutes. You've got a point, but as long as I feel in good strong contact . . .

DADA: Contact with?

DR. R: With Narayana, you know, with God. If I feel that my mind is one with Him, that my body and soul and heart are one, if I feel that presence, then I am happy. I think my research is important for . . . I don't know why it is important — for other people I suppose.

DADA: What is important to you?

DR. R: What is important to me? God.

DADA: Do you think that you feel the presence of God? Do you know that quality which is God, that energy called divinity?

DR. R: Ummmmmm. What is it? What are your feelings?

DADA: You have to find out for yourself what that quality is. Many people think they have a contact whenever they feel a little peace. This is simply a temporarily relaxed state of the mind, and eventually you are drawn back into your desires, cravings and ambitions. But is that God? Is God a little quietude of the mind, or a little happiness of the self? With all that quietude and happiness, where are you? If you really have a contact with God, that contact is going to change you completely. If you ever have a real touch, you will not be the same again.

We have many ideas and hopes about God, and the mind has built up some fanciful and romantic images of Him. But is that God? If you once experience that dynamic divinity, you will not fall again into the same routine, into the same mechanical trap of the mind. The new consciousness itself will show you the creative impulse of life. The discovery of that consciousness is now much more important than the hopes, cravings and ideas of the mind. Yoga is the state wherein you have that contact. Your action has to spring from that touch of divinity. Our whole purpose is to discover that contact, to be with it, and to allow the action to flow from there.

DR. R: I agree.

DADA: Then why do you come down to the level of thought activity and pursue your own likes and dislikes?

DR. R: Well, I think each one of us has to determine that for himself.

DADA: Yes, and how do we determine that? Is it a matter of your own desire and my own desire, or is it something intrinsic and fundamental?

DR. R: I am not at all in disagreement with you. As far as why, I think we just fall down.

DADA: Yes, but are we conscious of that falling down? And why do we fall down? When we once see that light, why do we go down in the darkness and get busy there on that lower level?

There are really very few persons interested in this basic science of life, and even fewer are interested in yoga, meditation and spiritual sciences. So we have to be very alert and vigilant to find and reach our objective. We have to discover that divinity, and be there, so we can act from there. Otherwise, we are just caught up again and again in this whole mad world — it is almost like walking on a razor blade. The world has its own cravings and expectations, and would like us to go down and work on its level. But we have to be alert, to discriminate in finding our best action. Our environment demands we remain on that mechanistic mental level. The whole purpose of yoga is to go beyond this thought activity and to discover that which is beyond the self. Yoga is not intended just to relieve tensions and pains and to make us feel a bit high about ourselves. All of this is secondary to discovering the union, the height, and we cannot have the idle luxury of going down again and again to the lower level. We have to show that new aesthetic beauty of living to the world through our own living.

DR. R: It seems to me that reaching that height takes time. Maybe I am only feeling the secondary effects of yoga, and it may take me many years to find out what yoga really is.

DADA: It is not a matter of many years, for it all depends on how you proceed. It takes many years when your movements are sluggish and half-hearted. It is so easy, so instantaneous, when you apply your whole energy to it. But we never do that. We see something, some partial truths, and then we fall down into the mental field again. Such a half-hearted glimpse may give the wrong impression, and will not make you capable of showing that pure state of yoga to the world. It is the mind that calculates, plans and aspires. The mind is very mischievous and cunning, so it has to be eliminated completely before you can see for yourself what the yoga quality of consciousness is. In the state of yoga there is no existence for the mind as a thought activity.

So how can you show this to the world? You will have to live with this thing and let it operate in its own way. You will have to discover that quality of equilibrium, that peace, that dynamicity, and then let this new consciousness express itself through the medium of yoga. Allow this new intelligence to act in its own unique way, to show the world what wisdom it contains. *Action and expression have to come out from this yogic state*, from the new state of spiritual awareness. The good of the world and the action thereof need not be the concern of this ambitious and clever mind. Let that true yogic state of inner intelligence take care of its own action and expression for the benefit of the world.

DR. R: I agree with everything you are saying. And maybe it is just my mischievous mind operating, but I really feel inspired about research.

DADA: You have to be very cautious about inspiration. People are inspired and intoxicated about many things. They get excited about hunting birds and animals, even about politics and war. Inspiration is not important in itself. And even if you have the ability to do something exceptional, you still have to look into this whole problem of capacity and of inspiration.

DR. R: How do you define inspiration?

DADA: Maybe a strong urge, a drive, a pull, a liking with passion.

DR. R: Do you feel a pull or attraction toward yoga?

DADA: I feel nothing like an attraction or repulsion. My approach to yoga is out of understanding what is necessary and essential, what is right living. Out of that understanding, right action follows. For example, I was not born for yoga or for spiritual life. I was a cricket player, sportsman and hunter. These were my inspirations. I got very excited and inspired at one time about shooting birds and animals. It was absurd. I had many other inspirations, hobbies and attractions. But I had to ponder, search and discover the right expression of my life.

What is this strong drive that we conveniently call inspiration? Don't you see that inspiration makes a man exclusive in his action? Such exclusiveness makes a person almost fanatic. And many fanactical persons through their exclusive inspirations have brought untold misery and suffering to humanity. Hitler was inspired about the goal of an Aryan civilization and making Germany a strong, leading nation.

Inspiration can be the strong drive of a fragmentary mind. And the fragmented mind alone becomes exclusive and fanatic about anything. There is nothing intrinsically great about inspiration. The inspiration of life has to spring forth from understanding and from seeing the whole significance of it. We need not have exclusive inspiration toward yoga and the mechanics of it. We are interested in reality, truth, the ultimate right.

For all these years you were interested in yoga. Now your interest is fading, and your mind is trying to create new interests. Soon you will have no energy left for this radical change, for this journey toward the height. The world is so apathetic that very few pursue this height.

DR. R: Do you mean that I should let go of my research, my mind, of everything?

DADA: No, no. I am not saying to just let go. I would like you to see the shifting interests and fluctuating pursuits of your own mind. *This is how the mind perpetuates itself, through constant shifting of goals in time.* It is the goal and the pursuit of it that creates time. Goal and time are fictitious ideas, mere falsities! Just take a little courage and an unbiased look into yourself to see how your own mind is working.

DR. R: Let me make myself clear. When I was in India, I felt I was interested only in yoga and serving God. I did not care about anything else.

DADA: Give a little more thought and see if you really are on better ground now. What happened to your urge to discover God?

DR. R: I still feel it, but I cannot describe it.

DADA: I am interested in that quality of consciousness which is beyond the mind, which works without any thought activity. This new dimension gives you peace, happiness and fulfillment. Are you at peace? Have you discovered that totality, or are you living through this self-centered mind activity?

DR. R: I had a strong inner experience two or three years ago.

DADA: Then are you operating in a different way now?

80   Beyond the Mind

DR. R: I was always operating that way somewhat, and my yoga teacher fostered it.

DADA: No one else can inject this change. Yoga practices themselves cannot bring about the dimensional change, nor can anyone from outside.

DR. R: Can you say that a seed only grows by itself?

DADA: These analogies are useless. They are exercises in imagination and speculations of the mind. See if you can understand yourself, what is happening to you, without any comparison or analogy. Take an impartial look into yourself and see if there is any basic change. Is there a total change, or are you working with the same patterns of thought and emotion, with a few amended ideas and values? Are you free from the pursuit of desires, ambitions and goals? Are you free from anger, hatred and fear? Is your energy quiet so it can enjoy the happiness which comes out of tranquility? Are you full into yourself with total energy? Are you a total being, undivided and unfragmented?

DR. R: If this happens, it would be a tremendous change in man.

DADA: This is the only change worth the name. All other changes are merely amended ideas. Such changes remain in the same circle of the mind. Why decorate the walls of the mind? The very tendency to pursue an idea through time is the usual old game of the mind. There is nothing new in it. So how different are you?

DR. R: I feel like you are trying to convert me into something.

DADA: Not at all. We are trying to compare notes, to discover the right action in life.

DR. R: I am mostly peaceful and happy, and I feel like the mind can be used as a valuable tool in the same way that a chariot can be used to carry a warrior to battle.

DADA: We all say that "the mind is a valuable tool," but this is an interpretation. Is there mind activity where there is a total change?

DR. R: When total change occurs, I think perhaps everything dissolves. But then in order to work in the world, to serve others, and to live a useful life, perhaps you need to mediate through the mind.

DADA: Only when you cease mediating through the mind does your consciousness and whole approach change, and you live by intuition. There remains no room for the mind as a thought/idea movement. Then energy functions in its original pure form — free, sensitive, dynamic and intelligent. Thereafter your very perception and language will be new. A spontaneous action emerges from the pure energy within. Then love and compassion for others become an expression of your total energy, and your actions are not based on any wishful ideas or on the conclusions of thought.

DR. R: I can see what you mean, but isn't it beyond the reach of a normal man?

DADA: What do you mean by a normal man? And where is an abnormal man? I see only two types of people. The first type is he who never questions to find out what life is, and continues with the inertia of the past. The other is he who sees the stupidity of the mechanical continuity of the past inertia, and realizes the bondage of time. Some get knee-deep in their own pond of time and stagnate; others see the truth of life and move toward liberation.

In this new dimension, the mind as a thought is not ever involved, even in the guise of doing something for others. The change is total, and the mind will not operate again. Whenever action becomes necessary, it flashes out spontaneously. When action is not needed, the person remains rooted in peace within himself.

DR. R: Have you found this peace and contentment?

DADA: I am at peace with myself. Peace is the state of deep contentment.

DR. R: What is deep peace like?

DADA: Peace is the absence of thought activity.
Peace is the negation of all cravings.
Peace is the freedom and tranquility of energy.
Peace is a state of total being.
Peace is existence beyond the mind.

DR. R: So where does thought come from? Isn't it a manifestation of God?

DADA: I will tell you what thought is. Thought has nothing to do with God. Rather, thought is like a dense cloud around the divine energy. Thought comes from imagination, from past memory; it is a product of past cravings and of incomplete experiences. When an experience is total, there is no memory and no thought about it. Out of unsatisfied cravings and unfinished actions thought arises. Thought has nothing to do with God. Thought itself is a diversion of energy, a hindrance to experiencing God, the divinity.

We must see the relation of thought with the vital energy. Thought projects itself out all the time and usurps our vital energy. Our whole life is based on thought activity and the pursuit of desire and ambition. What we call "I," or the self, is a huge cluster of thoughts, ideas, hopes, desires, and all the past memories. This monolithic cluster uses our vital energy for its own repetitious living. That is how living has become a mechanical routine. Only when energy is free from this catch by the cluster can it intuitively find its own independent action. Such total action of free energy is the intelligence of life. This action is unhindered by thought and the plans of the mind. The yogi is he who lives through such actions.

DR. R: That is all very interesting, and I understand what you mean. Do you feel there are some effects on the physical body from asanas and pranayama?

DADA: Yes, there are effects of yogic asanas and pranayama on the body. Body and mind are interlinked and do affect each other. The body is the instrument of the mind.

DR. R: Do you feel it is important to understand these connections?

DADA: Of course. That is what the first step in yoga is, to see this link and understand it. We have to be aware of and understand our body. We have to look into, feel and become sensitive to it. Experiencing is understanding. Such understanding occurs without having knowledge as information. On the contrary, such knowledge — preconceived ideas — hinders understanding.

DR. R: That is why I am trying to teach yoga to other people. I want to take people away from their thoughts and help them to be in the present moment. I want to find out through research how this "being in the now" affects the brain. I have come to you because you are very aware of what yoga seems to be doing. You personally seem to be very much here in the now, and you can bring others to this awareness. You can lead people beyond their mind. People in the West are interested now in the psychology and physiology of yoga. If we can collect all this scientific information about yoga, pranayama and meditation, we will be able to convince them. Your assistance will be a great help to society and to humanity.

DADA: I know, there is a lot of interest and curiosity now in these matters. But be aware of your own mind; watch how it immediately wants to collect information and data to convince other people. After collecting all such scientific and medical facts, what will happen? Do you think people will aspire to attain the state of being in the now just because you collect some convincing proof in the research laboratory? Can you change people by establishing a few facts? Can a fact, a piece of information, change the human mind?

We have enough information and experience about the futility and absurdity of war, but are we free from war? Every nation is still spending huge amounts of money, talent and human energy in being ready for war. Through a balance of terror we are trying to maintain peace in the world. Facts and figures have proved that war has never solved any problem, but on the contrary has always created more problems and suffering. War essentially dehumanizes society and destroys all human values. We have enough facts and figures to show how war demands death and destruction, and how it is a cause of disease, suffering and pain. And yet, our civilized and educated mankind has never learned to live without the threats of war. If facts and theses were capable of changing the human mind, the general dangers of pollution and the hazards of atomic radiation would have been solved a long time ago.

There is now so much information available about diet, nutrition, health, pollution, anxiety, stress and strain, blood pressure, heart disease and ulcers. The causes of many psychosomatic disorders have almost been established. But do you think man has changed through the facts and conclusions of the research laboratories? Medical research has now definitely established beyond a doubt that the major cause of lung cancer is smoking. And what is the response of man to this scientific fact? More and more tobacco cultivation on this earth! Higher and higher sales of cigarettes! Millions and billions of dollars are spent on beautifully made, expensive ads to induce and excite people to smoke. And the tragedy is that cigarette sales are mounting in all the countries of the world.

Recently I was on a plane trip to San Francisco. It was evening time. The sky was so beautiful with rich golden colors. The sunset was lively, moving and ever-changing. It was a living piece of beauty. There was a movement and pace in nature's play. This gorgeous and colorful drama of nature was being enacted by the evening beauty, just beyond the window glass of our airplane. But hardly anyone was aware or conscious of this colorful drama. Most of the passengers on the plane were busy smoking their cigarettes. On that beautiful evening the man-made atmosphere in the plane was smokey and stuffy. They were all educated and well-informed people of society. And I was wondering why the well-informed mind of man is becoming so callous about the facts of science and their effects on life. With all of the research information about smoking, toxins and cancer, people are still smoking merrily. *Isn't it the mind that is the problem, and not the lack of information?*

DR. R: Is it sort of man's nature to be like that?

DADA: It seems so. But will you call it man's nature and just leave it at that? Then how are we going to tackle the mind through facts and figures? We have seen how clever this mind is to absorb facts and still remain the same.

The human intellect has reached a paradox. The intellect is refusing to accept and oblige its own logic. The result of this is that the human mind has started living in its own contradiction. If you observe very closely the working of the mind, you will see and discover the paradoxical practices of the mind in its cunning and clever moves. There is hardly any consistency in the so-called intellectual and educated mind. Mind itself has become a mechanism of vested interest. The instinct of self-preservation and survival is very dominant. The mind has become a self-centered activity which is basically interested in its own continuance in time.

The educated human mind has reached a state where no further qualitative change is possible through facts and philosophies. That is why the best-organized educational system and moral teachings have failed to produce an integrated and honest human being. We need a new device to tackle this cunning psychological apparatus. Thought is incapable of bringing about the basic change in its own field. *The human mind today is facing a new challenge — the challenge of its own paradox.* Intellect surely has reached its dead end.

DR. R: I see what you mean. Sometimes I see my mind coming to what you describe as a dead end. But is there any way to proceed further from this dead end? I am working now on my thesis research and want to know if you would cooperate with me to do some research in the lab. If I am hunting the beast of the mind, I would rather have several arrows in my quiver. I want to attack that beast, not only with an arrow of facts and figures, nor merely with a yogi talking to me on the illusions of the mind, but also with a whole program of teaching and experiencing yoga. Some of us are going into research in psychology, so that we can have more arrows in our quiver.

DADA: What I have heard from you is that you are dropping your yoga practice and collecting facts and figures to prove the benefits of yoga. I question if this is the right way?

DR. R: I do not like to be led on; I like to chart my own course.

DADA: And what is charting one's own course? Everyone is doing that. And are they all on their right courses and paths?

DR. R: Each morning and each evening, I really question myself, my inner guru, to see if I am on the right path.

DADA: Now can you go a little deeper into yourself and see what is this inner guru? Is it your guru, or your own subtle thinking of wants and ambitions? Do you have real contact with your guru?

DR. R: This may be the flight of my subconscious. I will have to go into it to find out exactly what it is. I am glad we got through something! Now, as I am interested in educating the people about this consciousness that you are describing, I would like to have your help in establishing through research its existence with some concrete facts and figures.

DADA: I don't know. There are so many things people want me to do. I cannot scatter myself. For what reason are you doing this research? How are you going to intellectualize that spiritual finding, and for what good? You may find out from me the existence of a new consciousness devoid of thought. Then what? This very thought is trying to use that energy — for what? I am interested in bringing people to the state of non-thought. But you are interested in spreading thought, which is to give in to thought.

DR. R: It sounds like doing research on you would be like doing an anti-thesis. I just don't think people can change that fast.

DADA: Are we going to change people through the medium of thought? Only that mindless consciousness will set everything right. We have to consider the problem-maker itself, which is thought, memory, the mind. There is only one problem: the wrong utilization of this energy which is consciousness. Set the center right, and your life will be different. There are no problems outside really, but we are only dealing with and trying to solve outside problems. The problem-maker is here within, right under your skin.

DR. R: You are right on. I think the world needs you, and I feel the world also needs what I have to give. A part of me agrees with you, and a part of me wants facts and figures. By doing research, funds will become available.

DADA: Ahh. I see your point. Funds! Then we risk losing our spiritual basis in order to have something much grosser.

DR. R: The only reason I am doing this is because I think it is part of my karma. I have to work it out.

DADA: Not just by this so-called "working it out" will you finish your karma, but by understanding you can burn out that karma now, completely. By going through that research, you may be reaping more karma. The dissolving of karma is possible only through watchful attention of the compulsive drives of all the karmic actions.

I understand you; keep open to what I want to say to you. I see your concern for other people, but give a little thought to what I am saying.

DR. R: I understand that you are coming from your heart.

DADA: The heart energy is the right medium for doing work, not through thought, words or books. There are thousands of up-to-date books, but they are just dry words which the mind accepts. That has all failed. Only the living energy of the heart is going to work and bring about the real change. Benevolent energy of the heart affects the other heart to bring about the qualitative change, with a radical understanding at the center.

DR. R: Yes, when I was teaching yoga, what I loved most was the contact from my heart. I pray for a pure and radiant heart. Heart energy is very different from mind energy. And I think it is important to link that heart energy to the mind energy.

DADA: To link up the heart energy to the mind? What a big idea! Are you not imagining? First you will have to discover the heart energy. Otherwise the mind is going to play its clever game. Can the heart be in operation when the mind is active? Find out. Heart energy is not the sentimental or emotional part of the mind. Heart comes into existence when the mind understands all its illusions and cravings and becomes silent in meditative attention. Establish this meditative attention first, which is living in heart. You had that contact once, but now the mind has become busy. Do not just fragment the heart energy whenever you feel like it. I do not want you to scatter that precious energy. Why not make it a way of life to live totally in the heart energy?

DR. R: I don't think it is better to live in heart energy all the time.

DADA: What is your primary purpose — changing yourself and then the world? How should that change come about? Can you change people through the mind or through the heart? You have seen the sublimeness of the heart, but where is that ecstasy? Is it outside? Go with the stillness of the heart. It will show you something of a timeless quality. See its beauty. This energy will give you a new instrument for functioning, and then you won't rely on thought activity.

DR. R: I am interested in how the mind fits into the tool kit of the healer. Would it be valuable for doctors to learn meditation and all of these techniques so as to clear up health problems?

DADA: Yes, but doctors alone would not be able to clear up all health problems. Disease is mainly the expression of a disturbance in energy. Health is the balance of energy. Imbalance, which is dis-ease of the energy, causes disease. The patient will have to see the cause of the imbalance in himself, and by eradicating the cause, establish the balance. This is basically the work of the patient, which has to come through his own perception and understanding. The doctor can only assist the patient to find the cause; the doctor can be a guide and helper. But unfortunately, experience shows that the doctor gradually gets into the pattern of commercialism and ends up a professional man. He cares little for the education of the patient. The very education and understanding of the patient become a threat to his profession. The doctor has neither time nor interest in the patient as a person. He treats the disease and not the whole person. He rarely establishes contact with his patient.

Healing is possible only when there is intimate contact with the whole person. This pure energy of life which is uncontaminated by the mind will perform the miracle of healing. It is this energy of the helper that assists and heals. If doctors can establish purity and balance in their own living, they will find a new benevolent force in themselves to work with. Such doctors would become a very potent force of creative and benevolent energy. The very existence of such a person in the society is a benediction. That is why we need that pure life energy so much, that intelligence which is lying beyond the frontiers of the mind, that consciousness which exists beyond the horizon of the thought/emotion world. Discovery of this new energy is a necessity for the betterment of mankind.

Today the whole society seems to be a huge hospital of incurable patients. It is difficult to distinguish the patient from the non-patient. Everyone is suffering from one disorder or another — physical, emotional or psychological. And the touch of the new-dimensional energy alone will heal and cure all the imbalances and disorders of the person. The true healer is he who lives and works with this new consciousness.

DR. R: You can bring people to a new consciousness. It would be helpful to find ways to measure and describe this state.

DADA: First of all, I do not know if you have a machine capable enough to measure this energy, which is pure consciousness. This energy of life is free from all images of the mind, uncontaminated by time. Even if you succeeded in making a graph of this energy, what would you do with such information? Some other scholars would write more dissertations about this energy which is beyond thought. Clever minds would argue over the interpretations. Scholarly minds would find a new sensation in the mindless energy. So it is the mind that is going to organize, write and prove conclusively about this state which is beyond its own comprehension! Then it will have to prove some other fact. The mind always tries to bring the unknown into the known. The moment the unknown becomes the known, it loses its beauty and its truth. *The unknown has to be met with the spirit of humility and anonymity.* The known cannot meet the unknown.

One has to become the unknown to receive the unknown. To discover the unknown is to become the timeless. To know is to experience the state. Knowing does not happen through the acceptance of an idea or a fact. Education does not bring wise men. Is there another way to discover the innate intelligence? Perhaps only by diving deep into oneself, being quiet and attentive, can one discover this intelligence. The knowing of this elemental energy is a direct subjective experience and does not come through a graph or a machine or from a heap of conclusions. I am showing that there is a pure intelligence beyond the field of thought and measurement. That immeasurable and eternal could not be captured by the calculative and measuring mind. Only the timeless consciousness of inner being can fathom and measure the immeasurable.

The Artist

Expression

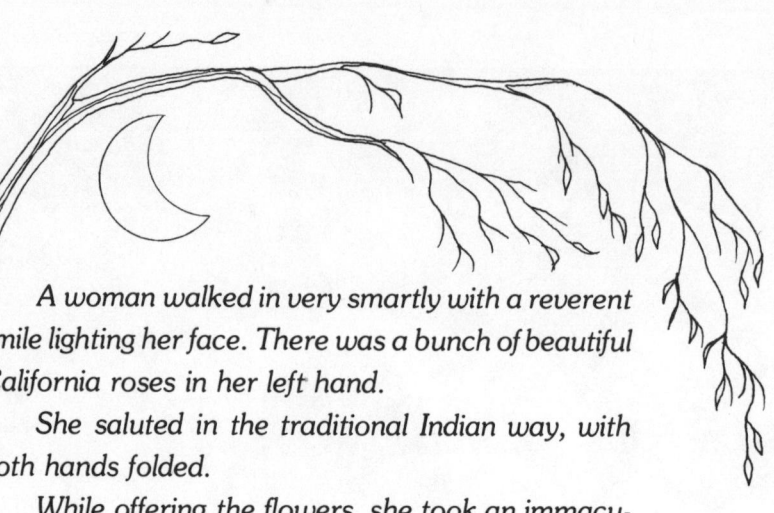

A woman walked in very smartly with a reverent smile lighting her face. There was a bunch of beautiful California roses in her left hand.

She saluted in the traditional Indian way, with both hands folded.

While offering the flowers, she took an immaculate pose, which was a mixture of Western and Eastern style. It was unusual, yet appeared harmonious and unique.

She looked like an articulate mixture of East and West.

Her eyes were bright and sparkling with innocence, and impatience was reflected on her youthful face.

She was of medium height, but the high-heel sandals gave her a few extra inches.

A shoulder bag with a batik print was hanging from her right arm. She was wearing a pendant of rudraksha beads, and a ring mounted with a bright yellow sapphire.

Her form and personality appeared proportionate and colorful with her choice of fabric and style of clothes.

Young, eager, sensitive and smart, she sat on the floor in a lotus pose.

6

THE ARTIST

What is true art?
How can I find my creative energy?
Are talent and technique necessary
for the discovery of creativity?

KELLY: My first love is art. I want to become an artist, and I am taking some art classes now.

DADA: It is nice to have love for something aesthetic. We learn to express different kinds of art through training. By training and talent the mind develops a capacity to draw, paint, mold or play a piano. Practice generates interest. Training develops the skill. Constant pursuit and ambition develop the talent. Clever people are generally very skillful and talented in their profession and in whatever they do in their lives. They certainly can do many things with great amounts of skill and efficiency.

But is this skill, this efficiency or this talent art? Is the skillful painter or the efficient pianist an artist? What do you mean when you say that you want to become an artist? Do you want to learn and accomplish something to get the recognition of society and earn a fortune?

KELLY: No, Dada. I want the real meaning of art. I want to be a real artist.

DADA: To be an artist is to be a creative person. To create, to do something original, something new, is to be an artist. Art is not an accomplishment, a skill, or an occupation of singing, painting or dancing. The expression may be anything, but the impulse within, the creative momentum of life within — that is the art. *Art is not the expression but the source.* The source lies behind all the manifestations. Unfortunately, we are concerned more with the expression, the form, and the technique rather than with the source. This source is the spark which necessitates the expression. Do we ever consider and ponder the source — the intelligence that lies behind? The form and expression may be fine on canvas or clay, but the source is much more alive, dynamic, aesthetic and sublime than the expression.

KELLY: Are not the training and the form of expression important?

DADA: Of very, very little importance for the true artist. Generally we are carried away and concerned more about the outer expression. Of course, it is good to sing a song, to paint a picture. But what is the source of all that? From where does that impulse of art come? That sound, that note, from where does it strike? Where does it take its birth? That which is good outside has its source somewhere within. What is the source of pure art?

When art is expressed, it comes out intuitively. It is a spontaneous expression of an inner impulse. That impulse is absolutely free from thought and mind. But soon the mind jumps in, to work with its plans based on desires and ambitions. The mind begins to make a commercial success of the piece of art, and starts playing with it to stimulate its own ambition. This mind activity is a definite hindrance to the pure impulse of life. Every artist should be watchful of this.

Can we be with that quality of art without the interference of the mind, and without contamination from the ambitious thought process? It is worthwhile discovering that innate urge and drive, which is pure, very strong and sublime within, and one shall be with that quality. If we are, then perhaps we will be true artists of life. We will not be just artists in some medium of expression, but we will be truly artistic in our whole life. Then every action will be beautiful, and every creation will be aesthetic. Life itself will become a manifestation of that inner energy source.

Then there is nothing like an achievement for such an artist. He lives as a very sensitive person, following the guidance of his own inner intuitive impulse. The work of the artist becomes the manifestation of these inner promptings. These intuitive whisperings come out strongly, with fresh expressions. Form, too, becomes new with substance. It is the timeless quality of the innate impulse that gives freshness and newness to the creation. For such an artist, every moment and every day become new. Being with one's own inner intelligence becomes the way of life. Being becomes living. There remains nothing like an achievement in life. The state of being is both the beginning and the end. In it lies the fullness of life. This is the creative state — the state from where all the aesthetic arts emerge. So the discovery of this creative intelligence alone makes a person an artist.

But we easily get caught up in the outer aspects of art, caught up in this ambitious, craving mind. Again, there is a trap waiting for us. Can we get free from all these traps and remain in that aesthetic state of being, which is the true art of living? Then we will be real artists. The challenge is to discover that state of beingness.

KELLY: Do you have any suggestions about how to discover that state?

DADA: You want ideas from me?

KELLY: You have obviously found something that works for you, which would perhaps work for us all.

DADA: How will you find it? If there were no one around to tell you, how would you proceed? Ponder and search; don't depend too much on others.

KELLY: I would probably learn the most by becoming still and open.

DADA: We will have to bring about that kind of stillness, that state of quietude in which we will be able to see much more of our own inner quality. We are not yet aware of our inner being. We are always life-extraverted, working through this desirous, ambitious mind. And that continually keeps us occupied so that we do not have quietude. It is the mind, the idea, that is all the time planning, doing and getting concerned. It is a game of the mind, which is just desire and thought activity. So as long as the mind, the thought, is active, there is no room for quietude.

KELLY: Can one quiet the mind through meditation?

DADA: You may call it meditation, but I am not interested in names. I am only interested in the discovery of that quietude and peace. In that state you experience a sensitivity, a beauty and a sublimity.

Occasionally we have a brief experience of quietness, but we are not able to hold on to it. Immediately the mind comes, ambitions come, thoughts come, and the quietude is dissipated. These thoughts dominate the energy and keep it busy with the mind's own self-centered plans. This thought activity is the negation of the creative state.

So is it possible to be with that creative quality, to be quiet, to be serene within? Then we can discover a new beauty of life in that silence.

KELLY: And keep it with us all the time?

DADA: Yes. When once you see that beauty, you will not be interested in the agitated cravings of the mind. You will see the limitations of your desires and wishful hopes which continue to keep you away from the creative present. The chain of desire and hope hinders the experiencing of the present. *Hope is the pursuit of thought in time.* With that pursuit we will never experience the creative state of timelessness.

We do have to act and work on the external level. But through the mind and its ambitious plans waiting to be fulfilled in the future, we remain busy all the time in the outer game. This constant outer drive becomes a chronic habit of the mind. Mind gets caught up in its own inertia. In this way, the mind dissipates all the energy of life with its mechanical and mundane drives in the outer world. Such one-sided activity of the energy creates an imbalance, divides the life, and makes one incapable of entering within. Without entry into one's own inner domain, one will never find quietude.

Quietude is essential for any creative work. Quietude is the spring and flow of creative energy. All that is beautiful and sublime emerges from that quietude. Ask any artist, ask any scientist. They will tell you how they create. Creation happens not through the mind or thought process, but only when thought is quiet and the mind is peaceful. Then some creative impulse jumps from within. That intuitive expression is the creative aspect of life energy. Only from the depths of the inner being comes out the action of the full energy, which is always fresh and new. This is creation. This is living in the state of art. This is the life of a true artist. *Art is an expression of the peace and quietude within.* You cannot be an artist without first establishing that inner peace and balance of energy.

Then alone will you be able to create and contribute something worthwhile to the world. Each one of us has to make the right contribution for the betterment of the human race on this earth. Only through such a creative act can you offer something worthwhile, original and beautiful.

The purpose of art is not just to amuse and entertain people. That is very cheap. Any buffoon can do that. But you must be able to give something creative, to lift the human potential of the people in that moment of joy, and not just make them laugh. Your art must have that touch of the eternal. With that divine touch, that sublime quality, your work will have significance, a beauty, and you will be a creative entity doing something worthwhile. You will not just be spending your life energy earning a few dollars.

KELLY: Living for a living is much better than working for a living?
DADA: Oh yes, we all say that. It has become the slogan of a mod person, but do we know what living is? A few desires, ambitions and the pursuit of pleasure is not living, but only a superficial activity of the psyche. So let the challenge of your life be to discover that art of living. Do you understand the necessity of that?

KELLY: I have known for years that I could find my answers and creativity in inner space. I also recognize the need to activate, to give out energy so it can come back. It is in that state that I get confused because I willfully want to do some things. I am beginning to learn that I should not do anything compulsively. I guess if I understand and have that balance, then I can allow it to happen instead of making it happen.

DADA: Yes, but you have to be careful to find out if it is happening that way, in that right creative way.

KELLY: We know when it does because it feels so right and is so natural. And we know when it is wrong because we have to tug at it, we have to go through barriers. I guess at that point we should learn to let go.

DADA: Let go, but eventually you will have to eliminate all the barriers that are blocking the creative energy. So how are you going to eradicate those hindrances to the creative energy? It is not just letting go; you can do that, but the barriers will be there again. How are you going to dissolve those blocks completely, once and for all, so that there will always be a creative flow?

KELLY: Reaching that silent space again?

DADA: Yes, but how are you going to bring about that silence? You cannot work through hope only. You cannot just hope for the silence to come.

KELLY: Do you only use self-discipline?

DADA: What do you think will be the real way?

KELLY: I don't know. Why don't you tell me?

DADA: You want me to tell you?

KELLY: Isn't that the American way?

DADA: Yes, that's the typical American way. You want it all to be told. (Laughter)

KELLY: Please write it down in steps one through ten.

DADA: Yes, one through ten! Start at one and end at ten, and then you are perfect. I wish that was so. No, it is a thing to be discovered, and that is the beauty of it. There are no major steps in that direction. It has to be the discovery in one's own self. There is no technique to get to that silence. Nobody can donate that silence to you. You alone have to work for the realization of this quietude. It is an inner experience. We do have some glimpses of such silence, but we hardly pay any attention to it. The easiest thing the mind does is to depend on someone outside to stimulate this silence in us. In this way the mind again creates a new hope to be fulfilled in some of the tomorrows of time.

Nobody outside can do anything about this silence. We have to accept the challenge to rise above our own self to the height where that discovery is possible.

You cannot get that silence through books, through knowledge. There are so many books around us. Now thousands of books have been written on this subject, books full of ideas, techniques, information, formulas. And after reading these books, where is the mind today? Is it peaceful, more sensitive, loving, humble, creative, ready to perceive the truth of life? Is it capable of feeling the beauty of life, the ecstasy and significance of living? Basically, the mind has not changed at all. With all the knowledge, education and scientific progress, the average human mind is just the same: full of hopes, ambitions, competition, material pursuits, jealousy, anger, fears and anxieties. Perhaps the mind has just become more clever, cunning and possessive, so as to function in a more subtle way, but there is no change in the quality of the mind, even with all that knowledge. The mind is full of information, but such knowledge will never give you that experience, that understanding. This new understanding takes place on quite a different plane, not on the intellectual or the emotional plane.

KELLY: I want to understand and experience.

DADA: What is that experiencing? How does it happen? Do we experience anything, or do we just live through ideas? Total experience is quite a different thing. The experience of compassion, the experience of love, is something other than having ideas about them. We do not have that kind of open heart to have the experience of love in our daily life. We hardly experience the near ones and dear ones, or any of the good things. We have images and ideas about them, and work through the mind only.

Even when you look at a beautiful flower, you just talk about it; your mind interprets it. You note the color, form, texture and scent, but you never quite experience the whole beauty as it is. To experience the flower is someting different than just to see it, describe it and mentally gossip about it. When you are really quiet enought to experience and sense something, you will not talk. The mind will not chatter. You will just be one with that quality — the flower, the beauty, the experience of life. Experiencing is a total contact of being, without the chattering of the mind. This state of being is the moment of creation.

You are sitting in front of me. I have to employ all of my energy to meet you and to experience you in this moment. Knowing does not occur by my making any idea about you in my mind. Knowing is experiencing, and experiencing is the contact of two energies. Is it possible for two energies to meet in the moment without creating the idea in time? The secret and beauty of life lies in bringing about this whole energy in the present. It is vibrantly silent and dynamically quiet. This present experiences and understands.

In the state of totality of energy you live fully and creatively. Then you will know how to meet anybody. Meeting someone is not just shaking hands, but is the state wherein energy meets energy, life meets life. In that present there is an intimate contact of two creative energies. This is a different dimensional state in which the mind is completely quiet and the idea activity is totally eliminated. It is the energy, the pure energy, that works, experiences, meets and creates. That pure energy is the intelligence of life, which functions in the right way. Then you are quiet, open, and yet dynamically active in this creative state. Whatever you do on this level will be artistic, aesthetic and sublime.

So, as an artist, you will have to discover the right artistic way of living. Living itself has to become artistic. You have to take this challenge of change, and bring about a revolution in yourself, in your activity, and in your whole life.

KELLY: If things are not presented to us externally, then what is the reason for beautiful people like yourself and other guides making connections for us along the way?

DADA: Oh yes, you are again in that "steps one through ten" business. But I tell you that it is not going to help you. You have to establish that quality within first, and from that state the external expression will emerge. But we are mostly concerned with that external expression alone, and we lose sight of our internal intelligence.

This new dimension is not a static thing. It is a very dynamic, active, effervescent and creative state of energy. It shall work outside. It will find its own external expression through intuition. With that quality, action will not be a problem at all. Every breath will be a manifestation of that energy. Your artistic talent will not be bound to the canvas alone. Then your whole life, whatever you do — whether you talk, or work in the kitchen, or play with a child — will be an expression of that inner quality.

External expression will be the manifestation of the inner being, the play of the spirit within. The truly artistic state of being is not a life in isolation but the fullness of life. The whole person is involved. Body, mind, senses and spirit are jointly involved in a unique amalgamation. There is no separation between understanding and action, or between intelligence and expression. The whole movement of life in the present is spontaneous and total.

He who works in this totality of being and spontaneity is an artist. He may work in any field of life, with any mode of expression, but a genuine artist will he be because of that quality of energy he carries within. For him, the work in the kitchen will be as meaningful as the work on canvas.

Art or creativity is the spontaneous expression of inner intelligence. Art is not merely a skill or a talent to be acquired through technique and practice, but is an expression of the inner being, which is to be discovered in the state of total attention and silence. *Silence of total energy is the womb of creativity.*

In that silence you are likely to stumble upon the pristine

beauty within yourslf. The beauty from that silence will be eloquent and expressable. You will then create beauty not on a piece of canvas alone, but all your actions will manifest beauty, art and joy. This energy of life itself will be the focal point of art. Art and life will be one. Art is nothing but the divine play of pure energy within. This pure energy of life is always creative, sublime and spiritual. This energy is the source of all the manifestations of creativity.

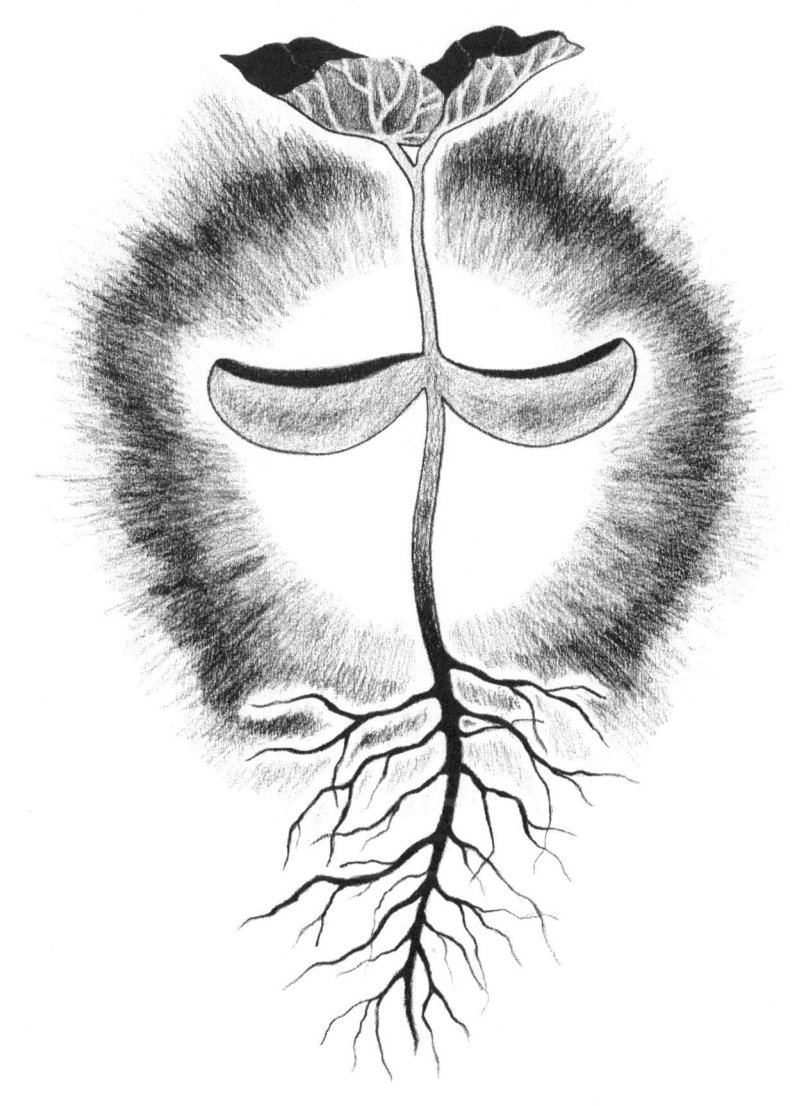

The Woman

Ascent

With her entry she brought a flood of energy into the room.

There was a freshness in her smiling face. The skin texture was smooth and creamy.

Sunbathing had added a little extra tan to her already-rich Scandinavian complexion.

Her movements were genuinely feminine, and the smile was affectionate and aesthetic.

Height and body structure were normal, and yet, a few pounds less would show her in perfect shape.

Round face, cheeks with a tinge of red, and a straight proportionate nose created an artistic three-dimensional effect.

Her profile was well cut, almost chiseled to perfection. The facial contour was pleasing and photogenic.

Behind the three-dimensional structure of her face there was a fourth-dimensional energy — twinkling, pulsating and vibrating to enrich and keep the structure glowing.

There was much more invisible behind her visible face.

It seems life dwells more in the unknown than in the known.

She brought a crystal prism as a present for me. It was a clean glass, well cut to reflect light through its transparent purity.

7

THE WOMAN

*Are my feminine emotionality and sensitivity blocks
to a higher consciousness?
Are devotion and faith necessary for spiritual progress?
Is it possible to be free from sexual energy?*

LEAH: I want to know if there is a special karma in being born in a negaitve polarity in the female body. At times I can become and remain the observer; then the female cycle begins, and I am like a puppet on the string of my emotions. I know these female emotions are a trap, and very much wish to overcome them, but I am aware that being in the female body has its liabilities. It is very difficult to master this female weakness in terms of the spiritual.

DADA: The female weakness? Is this emotional element a female quality alone? Don't men have their emotional urges and catches? The nature and content of his emotion may be a little different, but both men and women are prone to these disturbances and hypersensitivities. The physiology of a woman is in a way different, which makes her more susceptible to this kind of sensitivity which you call emotions. It is true that by nature there is a difference in the glandular structure and nervous system of a woman because she plays a different role in the procreation process of nature. But that is the only difference when you compare yourself with a man.

What is this element you term emotion? You have already condemned this quality by calling it emotion. Is not this quality a high state of sensitivity which the mind plays with? Isn't there an idea — the mind — involved behind this upsurge of the energy named emotion? What is this movement of energy when there is no thought or idea involved in it? Is the emotion independent of the mind, the thought? Look into yourself and see what this state, this element, is. Isn't it sensitivity, a very fine and subtle energy? This highly volatile energy is a natural virtue. But it is the mind that is playing with it. Your thoughts capture this energy for the mind's own fulfillment, and your memories use this for their own existence, excitements and play. *This sensitivity itself is not the problem, nor is the female aspect a problem, but the mind underlying it is.*

LEAH: So you think the feeling of feminine emotionality may not necessarily be a hindrance to spiritual growth?

DADA: Surely it is not. This so-called female aspect, which is a highly sensitive energy, may be of great assistance in the discovery of truth. Female sensitivity — the tenderness and affection without any attachment — will take one to the greatest height of creativity. Divinity or spirituality is the ultimate height of pure creative sensitivity.

LEAH: So then is it my traditional thought pattern that is affecting me more?

DADA: Exactly. Your thought patterns, your cultural influences and this socioeconomic structure have greatly contributed to building up this bias. A woman is physiologically and emotionally different, and that is a fact of nature. But when you compare a woman with a man, this misunderstanding or underestimation comes in. Accept your sensitivity and emotionality and proceed to take the next step. There will be no comparison with man, angel or God. You move on your own by knowing your full potential. Then your emotional sensitivity is going to be a blessing in disguise.

LEAH: I see this, Dada, and I am beginning to accept myself with a new confidence. I feel myself encouraged.

DADA: It is very important to have this sensitivity, as it alone is able to capture the higher-dimensional energy, which is divinity. Truth is grasped only in this pure state. The dull, gross and inert mind will never know and experience the divine. Can a dull woman, with a lack of sensitivity, become an ideal specimen of womanhood?

LEAH: No, Dada. Now I understand fully what you mean. The crystal is clear, but the mind projects unclear forms onto it.

DADA: Mind is the desire activity which is always projecting energy outwardly, extraverting us on to outer planes through imaginations and hopes. Can we rescue this energy from the domination of idea activity and conserve it? If we can, then the sensitivity of the inner being can capture something much higher. This divinity which expresses itself through intuition is the highest form of sensitivity. So, it is a great asset, but we do not know yet how to handle it. It is constantly used and misused by the mind, creating all the attachments through emotions and sexual activity. Femininity is not the hindrance, but this crude thought activity which creates desire and throws our energy outward is the problem.

Generally, this energy is consumed by ideas, desires and emotions, and is fragmented and self-centered. We are unaware of this other dimension of the whole energy. Yet we yearn for something creative, sublime and spiritual, but we do not know what it is or where it is, so we go out after anything that comes along, creating images outside to follow in time. If you look into yourself, you will find how the outward drives of the mind are wasting this valuable, sensitive energy of the inner domain. The secret is to contain this energy within, to hold on to it, and to be with it, without throwing it outward in the pursuit and attachment of little, mundane drives. *The problem of a woman is that she is unable to hold onto and live with this fine life energy.* This has to be gathered within to discover the spiritual height. But, through mind, this very energy is thrown down into emotions, stimulations and excitements of all kinds. That energy itself is a wonderful, creative flow of life. Without it, nothing creative nor anything worthwhile is possible. This sensitive energy is the basis of all virtues.

So, how are we going to discover the divine, the virtuous state — whatever you wish to call it? How would you set about to find this new timeless dimension, which is quite different from the mental and emotional quality of consciousness? We must see what the problem is; otherwise, the mind is clever enough to misuse this energy for its lesser ends. We have to be very clear about the mind, or else even your rich fund of sensitivity will not help you. Many people have sensitivity, but without proper direction it is used wrongly. Our own self can be very deceptive and can work against our best interests. Throughout our evolution the mind has become very clever in order to survive, which is what the mind's main interest is.

Now we have to collect this energy which is being scattered by the mind and emotions, and use it for the discovery of something greater. This qualitative change will not come about by following anyone or any technique. *The mind looks to outer authorities and postpones inner awareness.* You cannot find that inner silence and that dimensional change as long as you are looking and spending energy outwardly. You can establish this change into yourself only by internalizing this sensitive energy, by falling back upon yourself. This is the challenge of change: to bring about this energy transformation through watchful attention.

LEAH: How long does this take?

DADA: It is not a problem of time. You have to bring your outgoing energy back inside, and with watchful alertness allow the energy to act in its own intelligent way. It is not a matter of time at all; it is a matter of awareness. It all depends on your integrity and the intensity with which you apply yourself. Then you will know what a conversion is! Conversion is a dimensional and spontaneous change. When we stop the outward flow of this energy and allow it to gather, something starts changing within. It will happen without your knowing it. It is not a positive change brought about by any thought activity. It is not a conclusion of any logical sequence. It is a jump, an act of the unknown.

Conversion is not a mental affair. Rather, the mind itself explodes. This energy is a living and dynamic thing, and when it is collected sufficiently in the inner domain, it causes the mind to explode. *Energy acts upon itself to bring about this explosion. The mind cannot cause it.* Rather, every outward movement is an avoidance of this happening, a survival attempt of the mind. This spiritual explosion is the only revolution which brings about the dimensional change in life. Life jumps and advances only through such an explosion. We have to allow this revolution to happen.

LEAH: It is like the universal womb, just to receive totally. I am so grateful to see this. It is what I have felt before. But it comes and goes, and then the mind comes in. I see it is a matter of being attentive, without any method.

DADA: Yes, either you are attentive or you are not.

LEAH: It is not like an effort of the mind.

DADA: Yes, you understand now. And although thoughts will come around again and again, your new understanding is going to operate very quietly behind all of that thought activity.

LEAH: Dada, do you think that each one of us has to find this state and the uniqueness of his own being?

DADA: Exactly! I am glad that you see this in yourself now. Your understanding and the state thereof would not be the copy of anyone else. Your discovery will be uniquely your own. Thereafter you would live in your own creative and spiritual way.

LEAH: I see and feel the possibility of this newness. It is like giving birth.

DADA: Yes, this is the birth of a new consciousness. The old, the past, has to drop out for the new to come in. The new will always be unique and your own. Then you will have your own baby with yourself.

LEAH: How grand!

DADA: The world over, there is a need for the birth of a new consciousness. The human mind has reached a stage of stagnation. It can no longer solve its own problems. We need the freedom from mind and its various hooks and attachments so that we can gather the whole energy which alone will take the dimensional jump. In this dimensional jump lies the birth of the new.

Only those who are sensitive and intelligent will be able to bring about this dimensional change in the very structure of the age-old mind. To bring this change in the life energy is the challenge facing humanity. It seems the whole of nature is conspiring to drive the human understanding toward this dimensional change.

LEAH: The drive of nature is strong, and I can see that it may push our understanding toward a dimensional change. To stay in the spirit is something I have wanted for a long time, but I haven't known how to approach it. A spiritual teacher like yourself has so much to offer, and I am drawn to you and to your words. In the nature of women there seems to be a need for devotion. In the search for truth, isn't it necessary to have devotion to someone great?

DADA: We will have to understand very clearly what this is we call devotion. Otherwise, we will get caught very subtly in the traps and traditions of the imaginative mind. It goes after anyone who promises fulfillment of a goal in the shortest possible time. Devotion cannot be based on the pursuit of gain. Hope and desire negate the spirit of devotion. When based on hope toward someone outside, it becomes a commercial proposition. Is such a gainful and hopeful pursuit by the mind a state of devotion?

True devotion is not for anyone or for anything outside. It is to the life within. Such devotion, which is faith, is something innate. But we do not have this understanding. We see devotion as toward someone outside, which is a wrong usage of this energy. So you cannot be faithful to others outside. Such outer pursuits are ambitions and imaginations of the mind based on hope.

Devotion is a state of total acceptance. Accepting what? Accepting whom? Anyone of your choice or imagination? How can you accept anyone outside through hope — is it for fulfilling your ambitions? *Total devotion to the life within is the state of surrender.* Such surrender brings abut the integration of energy. Then there is no room for an expecting thought or a calculative desire. Surrender is a state of falling back upon oneself, of coming within with all of one's energy. You accept life as it is, without any reservation.

LEAH: I can see the beauty of accepting life as it is, but is not *shradha* necessary to find truth?

DADA: Yes, it is. But what is *shradha*? This Sanskrit word is synonymous with faith. This is an innate state of being. That quiet, alert, sensitive state within is *shradha*. There truth is conceived. The classical meaning of this word is: the state wherein the truth is born. In that state of pure sensitivity the truth is received. He alone is faithful who carries this state within. Such a faithful one shall find! He then will not follow anyone outside through hope.

The mind with its beliefs and hopes has absolutely nothing to do with faith. This is not a mental condition at all; on the contrary, it is the mind game which negates this state. One cannot be faithful to anyone outside of oneself. Faith has to be in life itself. Through such faith one discovers the totality of one's own being.

But instead, the mind creates a "point of interest" outside to follow in time. And in that following, it creates a separation and duality for its own perpetuation. It is very interesting to see how the mind changes this point of interest from time to time. The point outside becomes hope and ambition. And wherever there is hope, there is likely to be frustration, sooner or later. So let us discover this state of faith which expects nothing from outside but experiences everything in the inner quietude of one's own being.

Through proper faith one can find the beauty of quietude to experience the aesthetic state within. Then one realizes that there is nothing outside but the wishful play of thought. Even the images of gods, goddesses and teachers are all outside. Mind tries to follow them, and that is why one never has faith in oneself or faith in that energy which is the total state of life. That energy is the only reality. All else is imagination and hope, a perpetual play of thought and mind!

When you see this very clearly, you will be free of all the flights of the mind. You have to fall back upon yourself and discover that energy which alone is going to lead you. Therein lies your guru — your inner intelligence. You will be able to listen to the whisper within and take your guidance from there only. This guru never makes a mistake. When you discover this guru within, you will know what devotion is, and you will have the strength of inner confidence.

Then you will not have that kind of devotion which fluctuates from one philosophy to another, from one guru to another, or from ashram to ashram. Surely there are good people, sages and saints outside. But should we depend on them? I do not question their goodness or their quality, but I question the flight of the mind which tries to depend. Such dependencies and attachments are escapes. One becomes fully crystallized and molded into that mechanism of dependency. Finally one tries to find someone as an agent to reach God. A guru becomes the last dependence. When we talk about devotion, belief and following, we are talking about dependence of the mind. Because of this we are never alone, never free and independent. *To discover this final liberation we must be independent and alone from the very beginning.*

We cannot find liberation through dependency of any kind. We have to cut off these attachments, not because the belief or the guru is wrong, but so that we can see what is happening psychologically to ourselves. Why are we creating these dependencies all the time? We are interested in freedom, but in the pursuit of that freedom we are creating bondages everywhere. We depend on rituals, gurus, books, beliefs and routines. Then we discipline ourselves with various do's and don't's. Yet, even that creates psychological barriers, and those disciplines become a hindrance to our freedom. So we end up in a sea of dependencies.

Are any of these dependencies necessary? Do you see how your mind is the problem in all its wrong movements and ignorant flights? But we never look at our own mind and its workings. We prefer to be interested in others outside and in their lives and their glories. They are all really great and beautiful people, I know, but that does not mean we have to depend on them or follow them. Our own life is our challenge. It is easier to depend on someone else so that we do not have to take our challenge. This way we destroy our own initiative. We are so eager to take orders from others that we never attempt to discover what our own life is. We never allow ourselves to remain alone, to do anything on our own, and hence we never make this discovery. We have to begin with our own freedom. Let us be careful of how and why we follow, or we will always be carried away by the craze of the day, the newest fad.

LEAH: I am beginning to see how we are always searching outside, looking there for answers, and creating dependencies on people and ideas. Devotion must indeed be to the life within, and not to attachments outside. My mind is always wanting something else, someone else.

DADA: Yes. Only by watching very attentively into oneself can we be free of this very subtle and subterranean drive of the ego. We never see or question this thought mechanism. The minute a desire or thought arises, we have to look at it, and understand it, before it captures us. Thought is so constantly active that energy has no chance to move according to its own intelligence. Give your thoughts a long holiday and discover your freedom of energy.

This perception, without thought, is to see things as they are, without analysis, without any hope, and without any desire. Perception is just impersonal attention without any attempt to amend it, change it, or do anything about it. Alert watchfulness in oneself, in that moment, is a state of sensitivity which is not thought but is of the quality of meditation. Meditation is a quiet, polyangular attention into oneself. It is the state of pure sensitivity which flows in the moment of the present. In this state the energy is empty of all the belongings and attachments gathered through thought. There is no imposition nor any contamination of the known past. Without this fund of sensitive energy one will never know what meditation is.

Freedom from all attachments and desires through understanding purifies this energy. Such purified energy is a highly sensitive and volatile state of consciousness. But this effervescent energy is very cleverly used by the mind to play its own lesser games such as anger, attachment, irritation and sex. Through anger and sex we mostly dissipate the energy, and this waste of energy causes depression and exhaustion. In that state we ignorantly blame this feminine emotional aspect, which is nothing but a high voltage of sensitivity.

LEAH: Surely we do dissipate energy through attachments, little irritations and sex. But do you think that sexual energy, by its magnetic quality, attracts us to the idea of one man and one woman?

DADA: Apart from the magnetic attraction, one man and one woman is a social and moral concept. There is also a psychological aspect of dependency and security behind this idea.

But when one sees and understands the conceptual dominance of mind upon this sensitive energy of life, there begins a change, so that this energy loses its focus upon sex. It becomes very vital, energetic, effervescent and extensive meeting everything around. The magnetic attraction is there, but the mind very subtly builds imaginations and fantasies, and then grows on that attraction. It is the mind, the imagination, which makes the whole energy focus upon sex. That very magnetism, without the idea of sex, is the pure state of love. Devoid of mind, this sensitive energy is something very beautiful. Then this magnetic feeling is a living, vital, energetic state, which touches everything with affection and true love.

It is the mind which limits this experience of the magnetic energy. Sensitivity brings about the wholeness of this energy and the joy of life. We experience only a split second of this happiness and joy at the height of sexual excitement. But most of the time the mind turns the energy into sexual demands, dependency and bondage. Through craving and attachment, mind limits that attraction to the sexual area and to a particular person.

In the beginning there is just love, sensitivity and contact, and then suddenly the mind starts working and desiring something more. The mind creates its own images and ideas, and uses all of that sensitivity and heightened energy for its own ends. Without the dominance of the mind, there would be no indulgence in sex.

This state of the spirit is extremely sensitive and highly volatile. How are you going to capture such energy? Only through a sensitive awareness. Not through the dull, docile mind which is only interested in a few excitements. So we have to make our physical body, the senses, nervous system and brain so sharp and alert that they can play their part in capturing something much more dynamic, which is the spirit.

LEAH: It all looks very difficult, but not impossible. Yet, is it possible to be free from this sexual energy anytime in life?

DADA: First of all, there is nothing like exclusively sexual energy. It is the thought of sex that makes the energy sexual. Energy devoid of all thoughts, ideas and desires is a heightened state of inner sensitivity, which is the spirit. That energy is absolutely free. Sex lies in the mind only. The seed of sex is thought. And this seed sprouts through imagination and symbols. So if you are interested in becoming free of sexual desire — which surely is a drain on life — you will have to tackle this impulse at the very root.

To watch the thought take its shape in oneself is the right beginning. To watch and locate all the clever moves of thought, which gradually develop into desires, is very essential. Such attention into yourself in that fresh moment is going to affect the incoming thoughts of sex very mysteriously. This intense watchfulness is going to create a new state of understanding in which the thought of sex will dissolve: The further buildup of thought and desire will be arrested.

Such constant watchfulness is the price of freedom. You will then be free from any disturbances, excitements and emotional attachments. The energy of life will become less turbulent and more tolerant, stable, quiet and serene. You will feel the state of heightened sensitivity well balanced within, which will be a very dynamic and potent force. This energy is going to throw out its own intuitive action. This is the spontaneous expression of the inner being, which is always fresh and creative.

So, there is a possibility of freeing oneself from the catch of sex. The fact is that freedom from sex is not an end in itself. You cannot suppress sex or deny it. The desire for sex is a strong energy current, a living and moving force. You cannot stop or destroy it. You can only convert it. You can uplift this energy by changing it into its elemental state. Every thought and emotion can be filtered and converted in this way. Energy at this level becomes unbiased, free from all the contaminations of the mind, and so is spiritual. Therefore conversion, through watchful attention in the moment, is the way to tackle sex.

LEAH: You have helped me see some secrets of life in myself very clearly. I can see the problem now as well as the way to approach it. You have shown me the challenge, and have also given me the strength of understanding to overcome it. Right now I am seeing my weakness as well as my strength. When I take full responsibility of my total being, the question of male and female does not exist. I see now that the usual male/female polarity is at the lower level of consciousness. And the discovery of the total being in oneself leaves one integrated and whole, without any need of marriage as we know it.

DADA: Yes, the wholeness of being just is! And in that state there are no polarities such as male and female. There is a total unity and fullness of life. The energy is free, independent, unattached and unfragmented. To discover this state is to be free from all the cravings, dependencies and sufferings in life.

LEAH: As I listen, I see my mind becoming irritated. The mind does not want to give up some of the things it holds so dear, its egotism. I feel twinges of the lower self saying, "Oh my goodness, this means I will have to give that up." (Laughter) Certain ideas have become attached to my heart center. All my life I have had one idea: the importance of a mortal relationship. My parents told me I would grow up to have this wonderful marriage. I was married, and I have a son. Through that experience I saw the futility of that kind of fulfillment, and so I sought someone who was spiritually involved. I think people continue to turn to so-called "spiritual marriage" because they do not know that the total fulfillment of their needs is within themselves. I understand that if I am to acknowledge my full potential, even that attachment to a spiritual marriage must go.

DADA: Yes, I am glad you see that.

LEAH: I realize now that I must utilize this precious body for spiritual awareness. If I did not wish to acknowledge my full potential, then I could use this energy as I wish. A part of me twinges about this and is so sad, feeling that it would have been so nice to touch another being with sensuous pleasure and love. The agreements in the world in that area are so powerful that I have to be very cautious, due to my emotional tendency to sink into that trap again.

DADA: That is where one has to be very attentive and alert to see the subtle drives of one's own emotions. Only with this watchfulness into yourself can you invite the state of meditation.

LEAH: You make it sound so easy, yet I have fought meditation for some reason.

DADA: You have not fought meditation, but you are fighting with your feminine emotionality which you have already condemned in yourself.

LEAH: Oh, I see; yes, it is very much so.

DADA: Meditation is not just some mechanical practice. You have to discover what that state of meditation is, and then your feminine sensitivity will be of great assistance. The state of meditation is the highest degree of sensitivity. Activity of thought is very crude and fragmented, whereas the alertness in meditation is a composite whole. Thought creates the future, thought creates time, but in the meditative state you are in the timeless present. Through this gateway back into yourself, you will find fullness and freedom of energy, which is a state of sensitivity in silence. This is a great virtue and blessing in life. Such a sensitive state of meditation is your own, and has not been invented or developed by anyone else. This is your earning and foundation of life; accept it and be on this foundation.

The action of this total energy brings about its own beauty and aesthetic touch in all its expressions. Then one discovers a new quality of love which is free from sex. In this sensitive state one begins to understand all the movements of the mind. One realizes that this mind, as an ego, is nothing but the past experiences and their burdens. This sensitive attention in the present helps one to understand and drop all the burdens of the past. Then meditative attention becomes the way of life, and wholeness of energy and holiness of life are born. In this holiness of energy one stands exposed to experience the mystical beauties of life at every turn of moment and event.

LEAH: I recognize now that I have been fighting my sensitivity, and have not really been observant of how my mind is always creating problems. One can watch its movements and see how it scatters energy and plays with thoughts of sex, relationship and love.

DADA: Yes, that is the very subtle activity of the mind which divides this energy, although there is nothing like a division there. See that this "divide and rule" is a clever technique of the mind, which dominates and uses this energy by splitting it into different levels and compartments. Fragmentation creates a limitation upon this energy, and through this, the exclusive thought merrily plays its habitual game to perpetuate itself and continue in time. In the full flood of total energy, such exclusive thought will have no way to survive. When you understand this fact of total energy, when you see the beauty and dignity of this whole energy, you will not be carried away by the fragmentary drives of the mind.

So, sex is a fragmentation of energy through thought. In the totality of energy there is no sex, and therefore no female or male aspect. In this state life is whole and unfragmented. There is no deficiency of any kind, and no dependency or attachment to anyone. There is no thought of sex in the wholeness of energy. It is the mind which plays this trick by dividing the energy, by giving it different names. Through these divisions, mind conquers the energy and employs it for its own sensational drives. By being in this state of total energy, one can be free from the sex drive. The very virtue of wholeness, the very state of totalness of energy is the freedom from all the cravings, desires and drives of the mind.

This fullness of energy is the experience of love. Sex and emotion are converted into sublime sensitivity, which is the pure state of love. In the totality of energy the thought of sex is transformed, and the whole energy is internalized. With this internalization, energy discovers its highest summit. This very feminine sensitivity, which is consumed by emotional and sexual drives, can be gathered through understanding. It is the lack of understanding about one's own self that is the problem, and not the female aspect. This female aspect, which is a high degree of sensitivity, is a boon. It is a great asset. Do not make it a liability through ignorance. When the whole energy is gathered, it works intelligently through any part. But the part cannot work through the whole energy.

LEAH: It is interesting to hear from you that this whole energy acts through any part, but the part cannot work through the whole. Will you please explain this further?

DADA: When energy becomes whole and total, it discovers its own action. This action is spontaneous and intuitive. This total energy can find its expression through any sense organ, especially through the relationship of a man and a woman. But this relationship will be touched by a different dimension. It is the energy source that makes the basic difference in the expression. This energy will give the highest form and expression of pure and pristine love, even on the physical level. It is not the expression or the act that is important, but the energy source behind it. This action may be a touch, a word, or even a mere look. When the whole energy stands behind any action, the situation becomes basically different. The whole significance and effect are different. But the idea, which is a fragment of energy, will never be able to fathom the flow and immensity of total energy.

The Meditator

Liberation

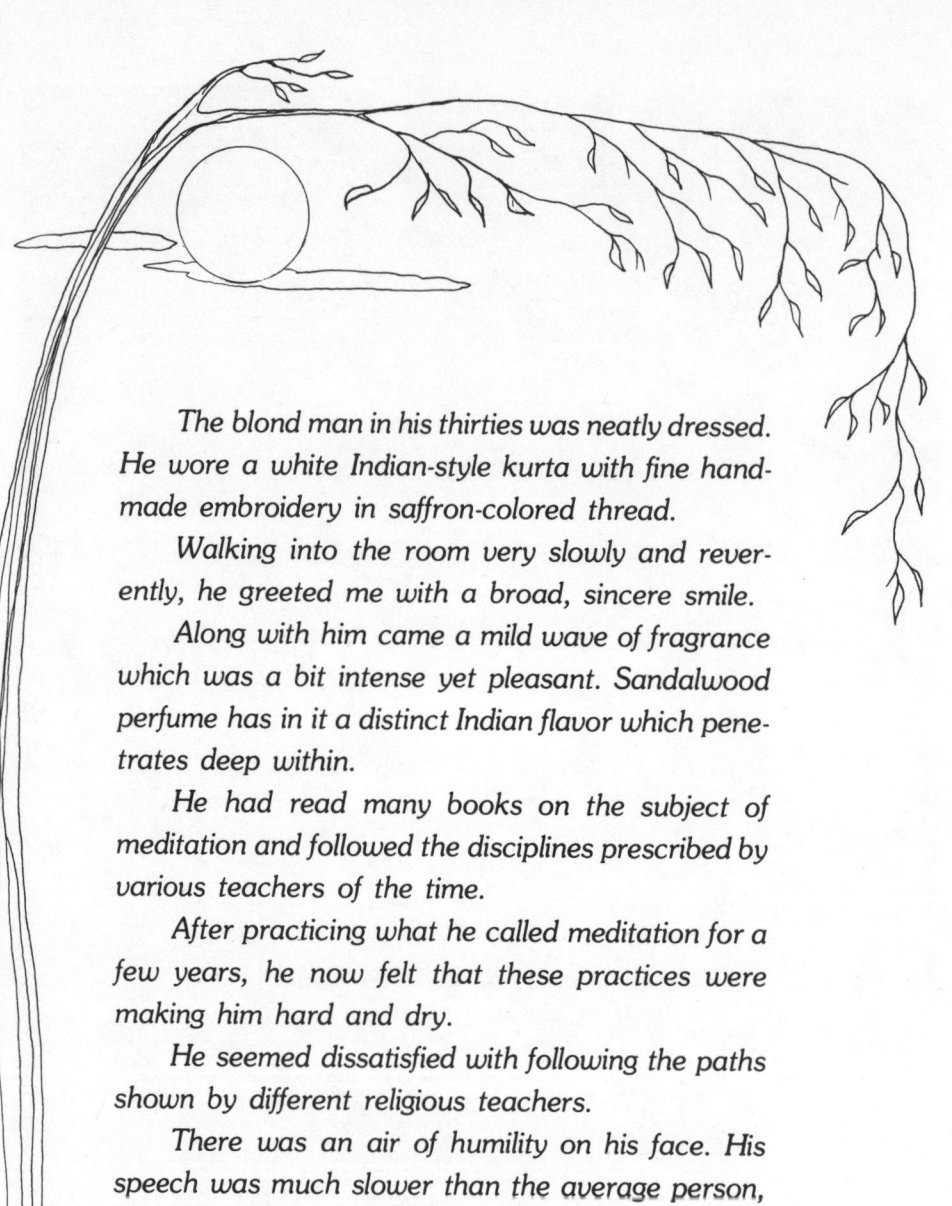

The blond man in his thirties was neatly dressed. He wore a white Indian-style kurta with fine handmade embroidery in saffron-colored thread.

Walking into the room very slowly and reverently, he greeted me with a broad, sincere smile.

Along with him came a mild wave of fragrance which was a bit intense yet pleasant. Sandalwood perfume has in it a distinct Indian flavor which penetrates deep within.

He had read many books on the subject of meditation and followed the disciplines prescribed by various teachers of the time.

After practicing what he called meditation for a few years, he now felt that these practices were making him hard and dry.

He seemed dissatisfied with following the paths shown by different religious teachers.

There was an air of humility on his face. His speech was much slower than the average person, but inside he was filled with many questions.

He brought with him a present of fresh red cherries and golden Washington apples.

8

THE MEDITATOR

What is meditation?
Is it necessary to live in a religious
community to achieve spiritual growth?
What are fear and loneliness?
Is suffering an inherent part of the spiritual search?

KEN: For the first time I am able to let go of some of my ambitions, and I want to dedicate my life to spiritual work. I want to purify and discipline myself to reach these spiritual goals. I have decided to join an ashram because there I hope to find more time to meditate. The plan of going to live in the ashram is making me a bit unsettled and empty. Somewhere in me I feel scared, and am wondering why there is such a sense of fear and emptiness?

DADA: Whenever there is a change from the established pattern of life, fear always arises, especially when there is a move to eliminate the vested interest of the ego. In all worldly activities the ego just continues on and on. The sole concern of the self is to guard its vested interest and continuity, and when this is threatened, a sense of emptiness and fear is generated. It is the emptiness that frightens the ego.

One has to be very careful to understand what this emptiness is, because the natural reaction to emptiness is fear. Man tries to keep himself busy through new drives in order to avoid this state. This prompts many escapes on different levels of psychological existence. In fact, ending the momentum of the past is the state of emptiness. Facing the unknown of the next moment generates fear. But there is nothing to be feared about emptiness. It is the most natural state. One has to face this situation to know the content and significance of it. By accepting and living with it, one can transcend this state of emptiness and fear.

KEN: Do you think that by staying in an ashram or religious community I will be able to realize my spiritual goals?

DADA: It is not the ashram that is going to bring you closer to realization, nor is it your house that will keep you away from liberation. *To enter the kingdom of divinity you have to become anonymous, a non-entity.* As long as you are somebody you cannot enter the kingdom. You cannot reach that divinity unless you negate yourself. It is the self, the mind, that is standing like a mountain barrier between you and divinity. You can erase this barrier with understanding. The place is not important, but the understanding which comes through the right approach is important. You can be in an ashram and still be busy in your mind. The mind only adjusts and adopts a new way, a new discipline, a new goal, and starts working in a new groove.

In the ashram or in any community living, the mind finds a new sensation and hopes to achieve its goal in one of the tomorrows of time. The priest in the church is not nearer to God just because he spends more time near the altar. Usually his lifestyle becomes a new regimentation in which the mind starts functioning mechanically. The whole philosophy of life becomes a new idea, and the mind just remains active through new regimentation and hope. As long as one's lifestyle is based on this kind of idea and the pursuit of it, there is no chance for a spiritual experience. Merely living in an ashram, temple or church is not so important, but the psychological state you carry within is important. By living in the right spirit you can make your home into an ashram, or you can turn the ashram into your home.

KEN: I begin to see now that one cannot necessarily discover truth just by being in a religious community or by making changes in external surroundings. If mind is the barrier, and if it cannot bring understanding, what will? What are mind and intellect?

DADA: What is the mind other than a cluster of thoughts, with desires, hopes, fears, ambitions and the remembrances of bygone experiences? This huge storehouse of thousands of yesterdays is the mind. It is the inertia of the past that lives on the energy of the present. Like the stars in outer space, the minds of men are continuing in time on the surface of the earth. This momentum of the past is only interested in its own continuance. The logic and cleverness of the mind are born and influenced by this sole objective: continuity in time. This mechanical momentum which we call mind has been developed by nature through eons of past suffering and strife. This inertia will continue unhindered until it is countered by some other force. This huge, ancient and complex structure of various paradoxes has developed its own peculiar logic, based on the built-in instinct of survival. The whole purpose and function of the mind is this vested interest of survival at any cost.

Therefore, the intellect or logic of the mind is not interested in the discovery of truth, but is concerned with its own perpetuation. Mind, the intellect, is obsessed with its own consistency and the validity of its own logical argument, and is not concerned with wisdom. *Wisdom is not the result of the consistency of thought or the conclusion of any logical process. Truth is the outcome of total perception.* Seeing the fact of any matter from outside as well as from inside at the same instant is total perception. Only the sensitive energy of the mindless state, through its attentive watchfulness, can accomplish this perception. The mind, made up of fragmentary and exclusive drives, is incapable of total perception, and is not going to oblige and assist you in the discovery of truth.

The intellect, which is the thought process and the logic of the mind, has to understand through watchfulness its own limitation, which is causing ignorance and sorrow. *Seeing and experiencing this limitation of one's own intellectuality is the beginning of intelligence.* Such a new intelligence which comes through polyangular attention in the moment has no personal bias and therefore is free from time. It is free from and beyond all traditions, cultures and dogmas. It carries a quality of universality within itself, as it is the consciousness of a new dimension. Such an impersonal intelligence is the outcome of the freedom of energy which lies beyond the frontiers of mind.

Intellect is the cleverness born out of personal experiences of the past, whereas intelligence is the movement of energy in the present, uncontaminated by the personal past. Intellect is born out of the bondage of thought, but intelligence is the flight of energy which comes with freedom from thought. Intellect and its logic perpetuate bondage, while intelligence liberates. Such intelligence is the beginning of wisdom, as it is completely free from all personal, cultural and environmental ties. One has to cross the frontiers of one's own personal mind and jump beyond to capture the ecstasy of universal intelligence through meditation.

> Meditation is the state in which you see the limitations and fallacies of all the promptings of intellect and yet remain awake and free within.
>
> Meditation is not the pursuit of any wishful idea or a thought activity, but is the very negation of it.
>
> Meditation is a state where there is no concentration of thought anywhere, but is the attention of sensitivity everywhere.
>
> Meditation is intense sensitivity of polyangular attention within.
>
> Meditation is the constant vigilance of energy in the present, concerning all mind activity.

Meditation is the way of crossing the frontiers of mind.
Meditation is understanding the whole structure of
the mind as it is in action.
Meditation is a plunge into oneself to fathom the
depths of one's own being.

But, there are some things the mind does not want to perceive and understand, and the one sure thing is its own self. When anything is seen in its entirety, without the sequence of time and space, it becomes a total perception. This way the total structure of the moment is fully understood, and therefore there is no problem or conflict. Only in total perception is the truth of the matter seen. There remains no choice, no hook, no attachment. And in this freedom there is a swift, intuitive move of intelligence. This spontaneous movement, which is the result of total perception, is in itself an action of the energy. Here there is no gap between understanding and action. The role of the actor is completely eliminated at this level. It is the whole energy that acts, and such action is complete. There is no room for reactions since there is no actor.

In this flood of the total energy of life, which is the highest state of sensitivity, there remains no residue as memory. Therefore, there is no chance for the continuance of memory as mind. The conversion of mind energy into pure sensitivity is the liberation of life. Such unbounded energy is free to act in its own independent and creative way. This energy is free from time as well as from personal bias, and therefore is pure intelligence itself. True meditation is the way toward discovery of such an intelligence.

This intelligence is the guide and guru for one's life. Let this timeless spark of the inner domain lead your life. Here is the path, the goal and the fulfillment. Then there is nothing like effort or striving left for the mind. It is the mindless energy that finds its own intuitive action which meets all the necessities of life fully and adequately. Life energy becomes total and pure to meet everything in compassion and love, and so leaves no room for any reaction or friction. Living becomes a way of intuitive existence. One lives on the wave of the present and so is free from the past and the future. Life becomes a voyage on the uncharted ocean of eternity. The wind of intelligence will fill the sails to give a ride on the tranquil and celestial ocean of eternity. To discover this voyage of intelligence and allow it to work in its own intuitive way is the beginning and the end of all human endeavor.

KEN: I can feel right now the beauty of what you call timeless intelligence. Man needs this new consciousness. It is so exciting to work for the emergence of this new intelligence.

DADA: We are living in a very crucial period of human history. Nature expects human beings to change a great deal. This dimensional change, which is the discovery of beyond, is the challenge of our time.

KEN: Yes, it looks very obvious from the present world situation. Life sometimes shows great promise and a sense of optimism. But at other times I get a strange feeling of loneliness which I do not understand. What is this deep feeling of loneliness, and where does it come from?

DADA: Each one is basically alone. Everyone comes into this world alone and from the unknown, and leaves it again alone and into the unknown. But between the coming in and the going out, each one tries desperately to avoid this basic fact. Everyone is intrinsically alone, but we refuse to recognize this as a fact of life.

Unknown is the other fact which we refuse to accept. Life hides more in the unknown than it lives in the known. How much do we really know about ourselves? How much do you know about your nearest and dearest? Everyone is unpredictable, and living is a series of unknown events. Every moment is uncertain, and every turn of life is certainly new. *To recognize this uncertainty and the newness of life, and to live in it with total abandonment, is to live in surrender and faith.*

We know some past actions and reactions of the individual, but that does not help one to know the ever-changing person in the present. This present is the only real moment which always remains unknown and unpredictable. Life in its true nature is always unknown, but we refuse to recognize this patent fact. The mind thinks it knows, and tries to cast its own dark shadow upon the ever-new moment of life. Only when we accept life as an unknown momentum of energy will our living become simple, honest and intelligent. And herein lies the purity, the beauty, the mystery as well as the strength of virtuous life.

Unknown and alone are the two aspects of timeless reality. To be alone, and to be in the state of the unknown, is to accept life as it is. This act of total acceptance, which is surrender to life, is the greatest victory. In this surrender one lives in the fullness of energy because he is not divided any more.

KEN: So one has to accept this state of loneliness to understand its significance. I can see now that this aloneness means to live without the reaction of mind. The mind becomes uneasy and doesn't want to stay in the state of unknowing.

DADA: Right! Mind does not like any uncertain situation. It likes to move from known to known. It is at ease when it functions in its established patterns, and the breaking from these patterns is the challenge of the unknown.

KEN: I understand that the acceptance of aloneness is facing life as it is with its unknown nature.

DADA: In facing the unknown without any reaction from the known — which is the mind — you become humble. Certainty of mind is lost, and the feeling of not knowing comes about, which makes one humble, simple and anonymous. To be anonymous is to live in the mindless state. This is the greatest virtue. This mindlessness is a fountain of creativity and is able to capture the whisper of truth from beyond.

KEN: It is very encouraging to see the possibility of listening within oneself to the voice of truth from beyond. One gains a new confidence to find that it is possible to awaken this timeless intelligence in one's own inner space.

DADA: Everyone has to face this challenge of discovery. No one can inherit this intelligence, nor can anyone donate it as a favor. But only with one's own attentive vigilance and understanding can one invite this timeless spirit of the beyond. This is the challenge before the human being in which lies the hidden blessing.

KEN: I can see now very clearly the challenge. It is exciting to attempt the summit of life. There must be something ultimate. But Dada, is it necessary to go through suffering and pain to discover this spiritual summit which you call the liberation of life?

DADA: It all depends on what you call suffering and pain. Does the explorer or the scientist who tries to conquer the summit of Mount Everest feel the agony of the strenuous climb? Does he suffer and feel pain in reaching for the highest peak of the world? Or is he full of enthusiasm, confidence and excitement to reach the goal? Does he not minimize the hardship, suffering and starvation? The climber of Mount Everest loses on an average of thirty pounds of body weight during the expedition. This shows the amount of starvation and physical exhaustion the mountain climber goes through. But does he feel this as suffering and pain? Ask any mountaineer and he will tell you how he takes all the so-called difficulties and hardships as part of the game. Is every difficulty and hardship a suffering and pain? The mountaineer, like a swimmer or other sportsman, is always ready to face the risk and encounter challenges.

The beauty of facing a challenge is that it helps the person to bring out the best in himself. These challenges and difficulties have their unique place in the unfolding of life. Is there such a thing as a challenge without the risk of failure? And what is failure but an opportunity and a stage for a new beginning?

As it is, mind is a bundle of various wants and non-wants, fears and ambitions, doubts and hopes, loves and hates. It is clever as well as stupid. Mind, the I, is just a huge cluster of various paradoxes with built-in inconsistencies. This is an obvious fact, but the whole attempt of the mind is to create an illusion of orderliness out of this disorder. It tries to find sanity in the crazy mechanism of subtle paradoxes so that it may continue as smoothly as possible. Mind keeps its vested interests intact through the strategy of refusing to look at its own workings. Whenever there is a serious attempt to look at this mental mechanism, it reacts cleverly and subtly. The mind does not like to be discovered and known. It lives and functions at ease in its extraverted activities. The knowing of the mind happens when the energy falls back upon itself by taking a turn within. But this inward turn is abhorred and resisted by the mind, as it knows that in this backward turn there is a danger of losing its identity and becoming annihilated.

When one seriously attempts to erase the mind to reach that state of peace, the ego comes out with strong reactions, at times violently, to hinder the attempt. The mind has the capacity to produce acute psychosomatic disorders and to disturb the physical body by producing untraceable symptoms. The ego then upsets the emotional balance and produces insecurity and fear. Through these subtle attempts, many complicated illusions and situations are created to upset this new movement of life. In this move of energy toward its center within, the ego fears its own liquidation and senses its annihilation. At the sensing of this imminent abortion, the ego becomes frantic and crazy, upsetting its own balance. And for the aspirant, these disturbances become suffering and pain.

Normally this kind of upheaval will cause a great deal of suffering, but attention within oneself, to note all the subtle movements of the ego, will keep the right energy balance and understanding. This understanding which comes out of a quiet perception will give you a new strength to accept the challenge of these disturbances thrown out by the ego. In fact, this very challenge becomes a great opportunity to develop your depth of inner perception. With the intensity of a disturbance — which is so-called suffering and pain — the attentive perception will grow. At this level suffering has its own beauty and utility, which helps one reach the intense and deep state of attention. The more the suffering, the more sensitive and attentive one becomes within to understand it. Suffering gives the opportunity to gather the perfume of perception in the present. And how strange, the more deeply you perceive the reactionary moves of the ego in the moment, the less disturbed you become!

This unbiased and aloof perception is detachment. Through this detachment you become free from ego disturbances. Here lies the way for one to get rid of the suffering and pain produced by these reactionary and illusive drives of the ego.

Then you will be able to live with this new insight of aloof attention within, rather than living only with the promptings of the ego. Then a mystical change begins to happen within. Mind becomes the mindless. Center becomes the circle. Insight becomes sight, and action emerges out of inaction. Silence becomes intuitively eloquent.

With the discovery of this new action, the basis of relationship undergoes a complete change. Our usual relationships are based on a process of comparison and choice, whereas the state of detachment, which is aloneness, is free from it. This state of aloneness is absolute, as it transcends the level of relativity by its choicelessness. Such an absolute state of aloneness is a point of transition. It is a critical point in consciousness where a dimensional change happens. The life energy being still, pure and dynamic awaits in readiness for its ultimate transition. Here in this state of absolute aloneness a mystical revolution takes place. This is the moment of breakthrough. Energy acts upon itself to explode the old structure of self, the mind. In this energy explosion the crystallized structure of self is shattered.

Herein is the death of the ego. And this is the act of spiritual revolution, after which the mind will not be the same again. A dimensional change happens, and a flow of new energy comes out to give the experience of a timeless momentum. One experiences a new state of existence which keeps one constantly in the now. One is then free from the past and future, and is always in the eternal present. This present is the beginning and the end of time. The timeless is the flow of eternal life. To discover this flow and to move in it is the achievement and fulfillment of human life.

Fulfillment

Building up of a Human Mind
Through Challenges, Suffering
Pleasures and Pain
Was a Great Achievement
Of Life Through Nature.

Now Total Elimination
Of this Complex Structure
Of Mind Through Understanding
Shall be a Great Triumph and
Fulfillment of Life Itself.

Dada